Return to
R. + M. Yarrington
Warsaw, N.Y.

THE SATAN-SELLER

THE SATAN-SELLER

by MIKE WARNKE

with Dave Balsiger and Les Jones

LOGOS INTERNATIONAL, Plainfield, New Jersey

All Scriptures are from the King James Version of the Bible.

Some of the names in this book have been changed to protect the individuals involved. The events are absolutely as described.

Copyright © 1972 by Logos International
Plainfield, New Jersey 07060

All Rights Reserved

Printed in the United States of America
Library of Congress Catalog Card Number: 72-94042
International Standard Book Number: 0-88270-096-0

DEDICATED TO
The two Naval bootcamp roommates
who told me about a man
named Jesus Christ,
and to
all those readers
who find this book
a road to a new eternal Peace.

Acknowledgments

Neither this book nor the Alpha Omega Outreach would have been possible without the prayer, fellowship, teaching, advice, or assistance of the following people: my wife Sue, Mom and Dad, Dave and Janie Balsiger, Les and Sally Jones, John and Peggy Hardy, Don and Loris Musgraves, Murray Norris, Pastor Tim LaHaye, Dave Lewen, Dick and Janelle Handley, Dr. Walter Martin, Blanche Mercer, Frank and Sue Morton, Paul Travis, Frank Foglio, John L. Sherrill, Ginger Studer, Bob Turnbull, Chaplain David Dunning, Congressman Del Clawson, Tom and Diane Speakman, Bob Larson, Pastor Tommy Beard, Bob Urmston, Karen Silke, Ted Lanes, McCandlish Phillips, Bob Bartlett, Francis C. Johnson, M.D., LCDR/MC/USN; Senior Chaplain Ralph G. Caldwell, CDR/CHC/USN; Lt. Commander R. H. Cain; Sister Mary Frances, Sister Mary Boniface, Dan Malachuk, Bob Carlson, Helen Hreha, Will Matotte, Sonny Arguinzoni and Lynne Wilson.

M. W.

Foreword

As deep as I got into occult practices and Satan worship, I never understood the inner reasons for people getting involved in occultism.

Since my deliverance from the occult, I understand the deeper reasons for occult involvement beyond mere lust for power—and the unlimited drugs, sex, and affluence that go with it.

A spiritual revelation to me on this matter is that a person is constructed like a triangle, with one side representing his physical needs, the second his mental needs and the third his spiritual needs.

A person fulfilling only his physical and mental needs is not complete, for a total person meets all three needs consciously.

A person who does not have Christ on his spiritual side is consciously or subconsciously undergoing a search for spiritual fulfillment, wherever he can find it—in drugs, occult worship, or elsewhere.

People seeking spiritual fulfillment in drugs or occultism discover that the experience can be very dangerous, in addition to lacking any of the peace and love so familiar to those who follow Christ.

This, in essence, is the simple truth galvanized into the heart of this book.

Mike Warnke

THE SATAN-SELLER

Chapter One

For all intents and purposes, and certainly for the intent and purpose of this book, the story of Mike Warnke begins in 1958, with me huddled in the corner of the big kitchen in our house in Manchester, Tennessee. I was eleven years old, and I had just been to my dad's funeral. The same people who were sniveling and crying all during the service were stuffing food in their mouths and having a ball, as if they were happy that now I didn't have a mother *or* a father.

Oh, there was Millie, my stepmother; she'd been around for some time. And now, all decked out in a fancy black dress like she was going to a dance, she kept coming over to me and saying things like, "Come on, Mike, eat something. You want to grow up big like your dad was, don't you?"

"Why should I want to be like my dad?" I said, not looking at her. Then finally, "At least, I'm not going to have to live with *you* anymore." I wasn't very big, but my mouth was, and the whole room hushed.

"Mike! You stop that kind of talk, hear?" Aunt Dorothy said. "You're going to live with me and my sister, the Lord willing, because Millie will have to go back to work, and she can't take care of you."

"I think you had better go rest in your room for a while and pray for your father's soul," Aunt Edna said. "This has been a tiring day for you, and perhaps you'll feel like eating later."

Not wanting to make either of my aunts mad, I went off to my room. I knew I would hear everything that was being said from there, anyway. Besides, I wanted to get out of my stepmother's sight. I was sure she had killed Dad. He was fifty-five, and she was only twenty-three, and trying to keep up with her had run his heart down. She had moved in with us three years ago, soon after my mother died. She and Dad went to Ohio a year later where she got him drunk and made him marry her. Dad was drunk often enough before he met Millie, but lately he had been drunk almost every night.

After they married, she beat me whenever she had the chance. Whenever Dad would leave, she would get out the dog leash, for no reason at all, and lay it to me.

Everyone thought poor little Millie was mourning for Dad. I knew better. She was just waiting for her chance to get back to work as a hash-slinger so she could meet more guys . . . that's where the fast money was!

My room was right next to the kitchen and I could hear what they were saying by leaning up against the wall.

"That boy's mouth ought to be washed out with lye," Millie said.

"Now dear, you can't blame him too much, losing his mother three years ago and now his father, and what with no one around here speaking too highly of 'Whitey Warnke,' you know. Instead of punishing him, you ought to be asking Jesus to show him the light." Aunt Dorothy was warmed up now, and everyone in the room must have been hanging on her words. I could imagine Millie's face when she said that to her. She probably was about to explode.

"Edna and I will just have to put some good Christian thoughts in that boy's head," Aunt Dorothy went on. "The first thing we'll do is get him to church." She said this with such authority, I knew I had had it right there. Still, she was such a likable lady, that part of it didn't bother me too much.

14

"I've got to be going to work now," I heard Millie say. "Thanks for your help and the feed afterward. You can take Mike's things with you when you go."

As soon as Millie left, I heard the old lady from across the road say, "How are you two going to keep the boy from finding out about all the shady deals Whitey was mixed up in? Why, just the last few months he was always carrying a submachine gun around in his big flashy automobile. I'm sure Mike must have seen those bullet holes in that car. The way I heard it . . ." And her voice faded to a whisper.

I turned over and tried to go to sleep. I knew all about this, anyway. Did they think I was stupid or something? Then I picked up something that caught my interest.

"You know that business that he started up in Tullahoma, near Lookout Mountain? Well, that was why his car was shot at. They were trying to scare him off from muscling in on their territory. While the car was parked in the gas station, they just pulled up beside it and started shooting. That's why he started carrying that tommy gun. Why it was a wonder—"

"Don't you worry," Aunt Dorothy interrupted her. "Edna and I will talk to Mike and see that he goes to church. We'll pray for him. Just because his father was no good doesn't mean he has to wind up the same way. Why, he has a better start right now than Whitey ever did. Whitey grew up on the east side of Cleveland, and when he was young he was already fixing prizefights and racketeering in the unions."

"I just don't understand to this day why our sister ever married Whitey," Aunt Edna said. "She even knew she would be his fifth wife."

I was glad Millie was gone now. I didn't want her there if they were going to talk about my *real* mother. She was the only one that ever cared about me, and she cared a lot. After she was hurt in the car accident, nothing was ever the same again. My dad was already running around with other women, and the day before Mother died, I overheard them arguing and Mother crying after he slammed out of the house. I could still remember what he said: "You go to hell! If I want to run around with the cute little chicks, that's my business."

I knew my father was fooling around with Millie, because I saw them together once when I had to stay home from school. Mother wasn't feeling good, and she had sent me to the store for something. I saw Dad and Millie in an alley, holding each other close. The next day I asked Joey, one of my friends at school, about her and had gotten an earful.

"You mean that nineteen-year-old girl that had a baby two years ago? Her stepfather done it. It was his kid. My mother said I wasn't to go over there at all," Joey said. Millie had some younger brothers and sisters, and they lived in a big old house hidden among the trees where no grown-up was ever around to watch what you were doing.

I could also remember another time soon after Mother died when I had gotten up with a sore throat. I didn't want to stay home alone, and I asked Dad if I could go with him to the truck stop that day.

"Yeah. You can help me gas up the trucks if you feel like it, boy," he said in one of his rare good moods. "Just don't get in the way." As soon as a truck would pull up, I would run out and clamber up the front fender to do the windshield.

"Say, Whitey, who's the new helper?" a driver would ask. But then he'd forget me and talk about what was really on his mind. "I need some more oomph to get over those blasted hills. Got any more of those pills you gave me last time? They got me through just fine."

"Sure, Sam, only they cost more this time. They're getting hard to get, when the cops come nosing around too much."

"Never mind the cost. I'll take the risk if it keeps me on the road long enough to finish my run."

I didn't find out until later that the pills were called "bennies," and they weren't supposed to be sold unless you got a prescription from a doctor. Peddling pills was just another way Dad made some extra money.

He also picked up cash by selling what he could salvage off of wrecked trucks. That was also the reason he was so friendly with the local sheriff, I guess. There was plenty of corruption in those days—just wasn't quite as organized in Coffee County, Tennessee, as it got to be later.

The day after Dad's funeral, when my aunts had me to themselves, my education began. They made dark threats about fire and brimstone if I didn't shape up to Jesus.

"Who's that?" I wondered.

They both belonged to the local evangelical church, and they were staunch, rock-hard members with an evangelistic streak that wouldn't quit. They beat me verbally as hard as Millie had beaten me physically, and they made me feel that almost everything I did and thought was a sin —which it probably was. But I didn't mind; matter of fact, it was kind of good having someone care that much about me again.

I went along with their views for the ride, to keep them happy and off my neck. It was a good life, and I really didn't mind having to work harder and keep clean and be respectful. And I felt good, deep down, whenever I did something that Jesus would want me to do. Unfortunately, however, I wasn't allowed to remain with them long enough for it all to sink in and for me to work out some balance. Just when I was beginning to understand, it ended.

In July, 1959, my half-sister and her husband, who lived in Crestline, near San Bernardino, California, gained custody of me. Needless to say, I didn't want to go to live with them. But I didn't realize until it came time for me to leave just how much I wanted to stay with my aunts. I even cried, something I never did in front of anybody. Aunt Dorothy was crying, too.

"You have to go, Mike, but stay steady with Christ. You are going into a Catholic home, and we can't help that. We know you'll be tempted, son. Just remember the power of prayer." Thrusting some gospel literature into my hands, she said, "Give them these to read, tell them

17

about Jesus, and tell them that if they aren't saved, they'll all go to hell. And mind your own soul, Mike. Remember, we'll be praying for you every day."

I arrived in California full of the words Aunt Dorothy had given me, and with the smart mouth my dad had given me. The first thing I said to my foster parents was, "Hello. You are all going to hell because you're Catholics."

My new parents did not exactly cotton to this, coming from a twelve-year-old country yokel from a small town in the Tennessee foothills——even if that town was the county seat.

Right off, they enrolled me in a parochial school. At first this seemed like slapping me on one cheek and then, without even waiting to see if I was going to turn the other, belting me a good one on that side, too. It was difficult to see that they were Christians, because they didn't shout and clap their hands, but went about everything so solemnly and quietly and in such a dignified and orderly manner.

I don't mean that my new father and mother were mean to me, or anything like that. On the contrary, as the weeks passed, part of me realized that they *were* kind, considerate, and a whole lot more tolerant than I had been when I walked in their door. They seemed eager to give me a good start in life. They didn't even object to my remaining a Protestant.

They drank liquor a little, which Aunt Dorothy had said was fire-water straight from hell, and my foster father was a man's man, rough in speech and quick with his opinions when he got excited. He was in prison work, and some of it had rubbed off on him. He could tell someone to go to hell in a lot of different ways, and use all sorts of hard language. Yet there was a big grin to go with that gruffness, and we got along good from the beginning. One thing was for sure——he never drank enough to get loaded, and he would never raise a hand to a woman. In all, he was a pretty neat guy.

It took me a little longer to get used to the Catholic church. And I never did make the connection with the

18

Lord or His Spirit, from whom all the liturgical tradition originated, and to whom all of it was intended to direct the celebrant's heart. No, I saw the rituals only for their own sake, and so they had a different effect on me. I dug the chanting and the outward appearance, and the emotional, almost sensual experience they created in me.

Some of the people I met at the Catholic school further awakened my interest. All that time, after the loss of my real parents, I was looking for a parent image, especially for a mother image, and right off, I found a *double* mother image. One of my teachers was the sweetest woman I have ever met in my life, a Dominican nun named Sister Mary Frances. The other was a 1930's Hollywood nun: she was Sister Mary Boniface, and she played baseball with the guys and was a stamp collector like I was. These two angels of mercy took me under their wings because I was the only Protestant in the school.

Perhaps because I had been excess baggage for so long, I was always looking for attention. Well, they gave it to me. I was frightened to death at first, though. I had never talked to a real nun—never had even seen one close up. I guess what attracted their concern was that I was such a hellion. I ran through the convent garden one time, in itself unforgivable, and kicked a divot out of the grass with my foot. I had to get down and replant that grass, blade by blade. But those Sisters really gave me a feeling of belonging.

It was the same way with one of the priests, Father Erickson, a young, redheaded man who had a beautiful voice. He sang at High Mass. But he had been a pro-football player, too. For both reasons, I looked up to him as an idol—but I was too awed to talk to him!

Because of these people, and because I wanted to please my foster parents, I did well in the religion classes. Sister Frances said later that I was the most avid student in religion she had ever had.

The attention and acceptance I was getting both at home and at school fired up my interest in the Catholic church, and especially in the ritual. Gradually, my interest began to focus on the mysticism of the church. When I walked into that chapel, seeing the impressive appointments, the stained-glass windows, the gleaming altar, the image of Mary, the images of the saints, the high ceiling, the dimness with candles flickering, the old dark plush carpeting, the polished woodwork, and, above all this, the finely chiseled figure of Jesus on the cross . . .

And when I knelt as the others knelt in that utter silence, then listened to the silence being lit up by latin and chanting, just as the church itself was lit up when altar boys in their trailing robes paraded slowly up to the altar with their tapers and lit the candles . . .

And when I suddenly heard the echoing of a hundred responses to the priest's "Hail, Mary . . . ," my skin prickled, cold chills tracked down from my scalp and along my spine, and my heart thundered.

The Benediction really hypnotized me, because it was the most mystical of all the rituals. I went to Benediction a great deal, and would sit there enthralled as the priests in their vestments and the bishops in their miters (peaked hats) spoke solemnly in Latin, knelt, prayed, moved silently from one place to another, and came on with the Gregorian chant as the standard was carried, that standard with the large sunburst on top and a *Host* in it.

It was Christ in there, just as it was the body of Christ we ate at Communion. It was *Him* in there! In that little square, they had Him. It was really Him!

And they would carry that standard with the sunburst and with Christ locked up in the top of it, swinging the censer, with the incense smoking, and my nostrils would quiver, my head go all giddy, my heart trip, and I would go into ecstasies.

All this really grabbed me right in, and I would spend hours on my knees before the image of the Blessed Virgin, another *mother image!*

I would pray to her and ask her to help me, taking my smaller prayers to Christ, and then going to the Blessed Virgin, to sometimes spend literally hours in prayer to her. For a while, my foster mother went to church with me, and

20

when I was confirmed—Yes, I was finally *confirmed,* and my mother was confirmed with me, but she stopped going shortly after that.

In the eighth grade I was enrolled in the Rim of the World public high school, but I still continue to take Monday evening, two-hour confraternity courses in the church basement. I also kept in touch with the church by taking two or three weeks of intensive studies in the summer, at the ancient mission, San Diego de Alcala, the first mission church established by the Spaniard, Father Junipero Serra, in his trek up the full length of California. We were given time for meditation and intensive courses in religion. The fathers hoped we would go back to teach and would be inspired to enter the priesthood or to be active in the church after high school.

During my first two years in high school, I remained religiously oriented. But I never did get properly grounded in the Source of it all, and so when I finally fell, I fell hard. Around that time, I started to date girls quite a bit. My parents were not against dating, although they did restrict me on school nights. They allowed me out on Thursday nights, however, to go to a gym. And sometimes I would actually put in an appearance there. But most nights, this one girl and I would cut out right away and go somewhere and mess around. There were many hideaways in the mountainous area in which we lived, and this girl seemed to know them all. And that's not all she knew. She knew things that made me so excited it was like being drunk. We tried that, too. It got so I couldn't think about anything else, and soon all that was left of my religion was Monday nights at confraternity class. Sometimes I would sense a terrible grief in my heart about this, but a thought of the last or the next round of clandestine pleasure would come, and my grief would be banished.

I knew that what I was doing was wrong, and I sensed that if Jesus was who He said He was, it was probably breaking His heart, but I just didn't care.

Chapter Two

California isn't a state, it's an experience. The incredible scenic beauty lures people to move there from all over the country. But once they're there, sheer beauty isn't enough. And to keep from seeing the inner emptiness, most Californians keep moving. A network of freeways has sprung up, enabling them to drink in the beauty at sixty-five miles per hour. Don't stop—you might start thinking.

My foster parents lived at Crestline, just off the famous Rim of the World Drive, eighty miles east of Los Angeles and a fifteen-minute climb up the winding highway from San Bernardino. In the summer, people from all over the state would come to fish, water ski, or swim at Lake Arrowhead. The camp grounds, tucked in and around the hillside, are becoming more and more crowded, and can hardly be seen for the huge pine trees that surround the area. This is also called the "winter playground" of Southern California, where one can enjoy a day of skiing on the slopes of the San Bernardino Mountains, breathe the clean, fresh air, and be back in Los Angeles by nightfall. A little farther, via more winding roads through lofty pines, is another famous resort location, Big Bear Lake.

From the Rim of the World Drive, five thousand feet in elevation, one can look down, through a gray brown haze, onto the sprawling, fertile San Bernardino Valley. The valley, stretching down the center of Southern California, is irrigated and planted in orange groves except for a number of fast-growing industrial centers. Atmospheric pollution—smog—hangs over the valley, marring the beauty of former times when gay caballeros loitered along dusty trails between ranchos, or vaqueros punched their cattle near some winter-blown stream.

The mountains actually form a semicircle. To the east, and northeast, lies the Mojave Desert, and to the south, the desert of the Imperial Valley. To the southwest is a plateau along which stretches the inland highway to the coastal city of San Diego, a hundred miles away.

"Mules"—dope pushers—know the inland route to San Diego, as well as the coastal highway, which they call the "King's Highway," because south of San Diego is Mexico, and south of the border is the marketplace where marijuana, peyote, and heroin can be purchased.

As a newcomer to the Golden State, I knew little of its colorful history, of Father Serra who established a chain of twenty-one missions, stretching from San Diego northward past San Francisco, the flamenco dancers, the Spanish and Mexican ranches of old—some covering hundreds of square miles of this now expensive land. Nor had I heard of the seekers of another century who scratched the desert for the discovery that would make them rich—gold.

I did hear rumblings of modern gold-seekers of all kinds, including narcotics pushers who followed the old padres' trails now widened and sealed as superhighways and freeways—hustling along with their contraband under the car seats or in the recesses of their tires.

As I listened to the stories of these purveyors of the flower faith who were at that time just starting to found their communal missions in out-of-the-way places between the missions of old, something deep within me stirred, then awaited germination.

At that time, the "good" boys and girls took the westerly trail eighty miles across the broad San Bernardino Valley, over the coastal ranges, and, zoom, down to the beaches for ocean swimming, surfing, and sunbathing.

Once in a while, some of us would go southeast into the desert for a date at world-famous Palm Springs, just to be near the famous movie people who flocked there.

The distance we traveled just to do something different was only one of the reasons my parents were having a hard time keeping track of me. School activities, dates, and church meetings at night began to keep me away from home more and more. The high school was only a fifteen-minute drive from Crestline, built right into the side of the mountain. You might say it was a good jumping-off place for going on to other activities. Like most teen-agers, I didn't want to call home to tell my parents were I was headed, especially if something came up at the last minute like, "Let's stop in at that new place that just opened at Arrowhead. I hear they have some groovy music there!" That's how I spent my junior year and the following summer. Somebody always had a car, and we would drive fifty miles for a double-decker hamburger.

By the time school started again, I began to set a different pattern. I had noticed a certain girl by the name of Carol, and she seemed to have a lot of friends. She and her friend Sue dated fellows like the captain of the football team, and they always went to the big dances and parties with the "good" or straight guys. I tried to attract their attention and even went out of my way to ask for a date but got turned down. From then on I gave them the cold shoulder. I thought they were a bunch of snobs anyway and as much as told told them so. Football players—I was tougher than any of them, of that I was certain. I showed my indifference by starting to drink more and running with the somewhat "rougher" set all the time now.

It was soon apparent to everyone that school was no longer important to me, and my dad and mom began to get on my back about it. Our conversations became one-sided arguments according to me, with Dad always yelling that I did not do this or that, and why didn't I get my hair cut? This seemed to irritate him the most. My hair was not really that long then, but it was definitely longer than his. When Dad would finish, Mother would start in on me about studying more and picking up after myself, and not looking like such a creep. I would just stomp off, thinking they did not understand me—which gave me a perfect excuse to drink more.

By the time I graduated from the Rim of the World High School, I had a genuine full-scale drinking problem. And I had discovered a whole new world—a world of freedom, lots of girls, plenty of booze, and no more nag, nag, nag from my parents.

I started frequenting those coffeehouses where I was not "different" from the rest of the gang—unless I wanted to be. Most all of these places played folk songs. You could go into these coffeehouses, sit, relax, and meet people if you wanted. Otherwise, you could just sit there and listen to the sounds.

The one I really went for was the Penny University in San Bernardino. "Old Penny U," we used to call it. I hung around there quite a bit and got acquainted with the owner. For eight months I pretended I was an Englishman. I got pretty good at imitating the accent, too. I don't know why I did it; I guess it just sounded sort of big. I liked the guitar player, who was black, and I danced with a black girl named Angela frequently. Friends there would get me all the hard liquor I wanted, and I did not have to pretend with them. We could all just be ourselves—no questions asked. I stayed there as much as possible to be out of my parents' hair.

That summer Mom and Dad suggested I go back to Tennessee and visit all my relatives I had not seen since coming to California. I was due to start college in the fall, and maybe they thought it would sober me up a little. Why not? I was bored out of my skull as it was, and it would be something to do.

Seeing my relatives and some of the hard places they lived, compared with California and the easy life I had been having, made me realize how much I liked it where I was. I never admitted it to my parents, but I was glad to get back. Knowing I had only two more weeks before college started, I stayed out of everyone's way as much as possible.

I began to talk about things more with others my age, guys who went to "different" churches or none at all. They did not seem too fazed by church, one way or another. But the memories of my earlier upbringing, of the aunts who had tried to teach me to ask God directly for help, suddenly began coming back and wouldn't quit. I started bugging my religion teachers with these doubts, and irritated them no end.

"Why can't we talk to God directly?" I would ask. "My aunts used to ask God for help, get down on their knees and pray right to Him. And they used to tell me about some of the answers that they got from prayer. And I'll tell you something: it worked."

Another thing bothering me was the fact that there were so many right in our own parish that needed help, while there was always a constant drive for money going on. I remember this one kid whose parents did all they could to scrape up the tuition to send him to school. He was a hyperthyroid case, needed glasses, and his clothes looked as if they had been pieced together. Where was all this money going? Why was it not used to help the kids in this family? We were driven to church on Sunday in a nice big car, threw a bunch of money in the collection plate, and where did it go?

When I enrolled in confraternity class in San Bernardino, I was armed with these questions and not content to keep my mouth shut. Most of our classes on religion were very informal, and it gave us a chance to really dig in, study, ask questions, and talk with the priests. The majority of the teenagers who went to confraternity classes were getting something out of it as well as believing everything they were told. The longer I sat in class, listening and talking about their doctrine, the more I began to squirm. The activities they had planned for us seemed dull compared to what I had been doing in high school. Even the girls looked kind of square—you know, the Goody-Two-shoes kind.

I guess I asked a few too many belligerent questions without waiting for an answer. At least, the priests did not get the feeling I was there to learn, but merely a restless, doubting kid, wanting to make trouble. They put up with me for a week.

At the end of that week, the Father Rector asked me to leave and not to come back. I got the usual lecture concerning the time they had been spending with me, the great hopes they had had for me, the good student I *had* appeared to be, and what had happened?

I didn't have any answers for him. I was just glad to leave. I was beginning to wonder why I had spent so much time in religion classes and seminaries, letting them try to groom me for the priesthood, when my heart was no longer in it. I was not one to sit around and feel sorry for myself. Not me, not the son of Whitey Warnke!

The last week of the summer before college I spent in showing that I did not care what the church thought. By now I had found another more interesting group of friends.

When a friend asked me to come up and stay with him while I was going to college, I took him up on it right away. In fact, I moved in a little early, telling Mom and Dad that I wanted to get settled before college started.

San Bernardino Valley College has an incredibly beautiful setting. You can walk along the tree-lined quad or lie on the sweet grass and watch the girls go by. The campus is surrounded by trees, and the buildings blend in with the landscape with lots of ivy growing up their sides. It looks like a campus should look.

My roommate, Herb Taylor, did not exactly help me stay off the bottle; in fact, he turned out to be another teenage alcoholic, equally glad to get away from home. Playing pass-the-bottle, we passed the time until college started with comparisons of our over-strict parents, our need to be independent, and how unwanted and boxed-in we felt at home.

Before I started college, I went to the Salvation Army and the Goodwill stores and bought some clothes. My hair was down to my collar by now, and the outfits that I picked up went perfectly with long hair. I bought an old 1920's suit, several spotted shirts, weird pants, and anything I could get my hands on that looked different. My favorite outfit was this blanket sewn up on either side. That really attracted attention. Most of the attention came from the chicks, and needless to say, I did not turn it down.

College began with the usual registration and standing in line to sign up for this or that class. When Freshman Day came, I put on my special garb. Now I was really one of the guys—hip! The professors looked at me a bit strangely, probably wondering what to expect next.

We sat and listened to the president's speech to the student body: "The main end of education is to enliven the individual to the importance of being and believing rather than merely doing. The development of citizenship and civic participation are important, but the development of the whole person is the broader and main goal of the college."

"Well," I thought to myself, "I've come to the right place."

Nothing else he said in that hour-long speech seemed new, except the fact that we were to strive to work out a personal philosophy of life which would be in harmony with factors affecting one's life. This seemed to fit in with my philosophy at the moment.

Before I knew it, I was signed up and starting classes in U.S. history, political science, English, and physical education. I was hoping to get into a philosophy course right away, but that was not open to first-term freshmen.

I attended classes regularly at first, but I wasn't about to cut down on my drinking. As the days went by, it became harder to concentrate on what the professors were saying, but I could still talk my way out of anything, and this carried me through. I was drinking so much by now, it was starting to wreck my stomach, and sometimes I would have to leave the classroom to get something to drink.

One morning, after an especially bad night, I literally

could not hold my head up. I had to leave class and barely made it out to the lawn before vomiting my insides up. When I was through, sitting there, trying to get my breath and forget about the awful taste, there was this guy looking down at me.

"You know, you're killing yourself on alcohol," he said. "Don't you know what booze does to you inside? Wait till you're barfing like that every day—if you're not already." I frowned and tried to think of something to put him down with, but instead of going on with his lecture, he looked around and then said, "Look, I've got what you need." He sat down beside me an pulled out a pack of unlabeled cigarettes.

Now this guy did not look like the dirty old man wearing a raincoat who molested little children on a bus. He was a real smart dresser, just a regular college student who wore a pin-striped shirt with the button-down collar, levis, and black tennis shoes. His name was Dean Armstrong.

"What's that?" I asked.

"Marijuana."

"Man, you must be nuts." Well, I just brushed him off. Got up and split. You know, back in 1965 anybody that smoked a reefer, had his hair slicked back, wore a black leather jacket with chains on it, and carried a switchblade —ugh! That kind of jazz turned me off.

It was about this time that I switched roommates. A week or so went by, and my stomach was still hurting. I tried everything I could think of, except giving up drinking. My new roommate suggested I try what Dean had offered me, and not wanting to be left out, I finally went along with it.

Classes started getting more interesting again, and I got to where I really liked marijuana. My stomach was much better when I laid off the liquor, and by substituting marijuana, I began to feel good again.

I made a return trip to the Salvation Army and bought some black pants and freaky shirts. My hair was longer than ever, and I bleached it blond. I was really craving attention, and I got it. You know, weird people attract chicks. That's why you hear about more girls running away than boys.

For some reason, my ability to slick-talk had stuck with me, and I used it more and more in my classes. Most of my friends were the pseudo-intellectual type. We liked to lie out on the lawn in the quad after classes and discuss psychology, philosophy, religion, art, and politics. Other students began coming around, and they seemed to look to me for answers to their questions. Anything I said was okay with them. And it was certainly okay with me. If they were that hung up for a leader, I was happy to oblige.

It was not long before someone introduced me to peyote, which had been brought up from Mexico. By this time I was smoking pot like mad, turning on in the morning, at noon, and when I got home from classes. I was really starting to live, I thought. All these good-looking chicks coming around, everybody listening to what I had to say. My days as an outsider were over!

When we tried the peyote, we decided it was better and heavier than pot. We also started eating mescaline in our food in increasing quantities, and from there we went on to reds.

The marijuana had been free to start with, then Dean started giving it to me at a buck a load. In San Bernardino there was not much of a market in those days, so most of the pushers practically gave the stuff away until they were sure someone was hooked psychologically. By the time we got to the heavier stuff, it was harder to get and the cost went up.

Soon after, word got around the quad that a Harvard psychologist named Leary had come out with a treatise on LSD. Some doctors came to the campus to conduct controlled group experiments on the drug. My friends and I decided to volunteer for the tests.

I thought the whole idea was kind of scary, but I knew it would be something different, and at that time I was looking for anything that was different.

After you go through the first stages of the dilated pupils, the faster heartbeat, a feeling of coldness, your sight becomes blurred, and your depth perception makes like an accordion the doctor held something up for us to see, and it looked far away, then close. I even began to "hear" different objects! They told us later that a person's sensations may "cross over," like you might *see* sound and music as a pattern or color instead of hearing it. And not only are your senses jumbled up, but all of nature's safety valves are tied down, and you begin to hear conversations far away and feel the faintest vibrations vastly amplified. All of which is exciting at first, but then you'd like to shut it off, only you can't. And that's when acid gets hairy.

My first trips were pleasant enough. On one, I felt as if I had left my body and met only people who really liked me for what I was. But one of the final experimental tests was a different experience. After seeing many strange noises, I imagined my insides were floating like feathers away from me into an empty space. In desperation I kept trying to grasp at these parts, always slipping just as I was about to grab my heart. It was sheer, wide-open horror—and it didn't stop.

We know now that flashbacks which occur after a bad LSD trip have caused quite a few deaths. A flashback can plunge one back into a horrifying experience as much as six months or even a year later, and can convince a person that he is going insane. Diane Linkletter's death was the direct result of a bad flashback.

Had the doctors warned us of flashbacks and other possible side effects of this drug, we probably would have taken it anyway. Had I known that 85 percent of the people who go on to other drugs start with marijuana, would I have tried the LSD experiment? I'm afraid so. Granted, they did not know then what could happen on a bad trip, but the point is, I did not even ask questions. I just sat there and let them shove it into me. Where was the question man? Where was the boy who insisted on knowing all the answers before he could or would make up his mind to do something?

When I went off to college, I was told that this would be

31

the place where I could learn to expand my mind, be exposed to new ideas and different ways of living. College certainly did all of that. I was taking these new "ideas" and turning them the way I wanted them to go. Even after the LSD experiments were over, a few of us kept on using it.

Word got around fast that I would try anything, and it was not long before I was asked by a bunch of fellows I had seen around campus to be their guest at a party. This crowd was different from the people I had been hanging around with. Most of them were older, and I was flattered that they would want to include me in their fun. Their chicks were more with it—had a certain look about them that was somewhat mysterious.

The party got off to a slow start, but as the evening progressed I noticed several of the students ducking into another room. After a while they would drift back in, staring into space. Then, as the room started getting more crowded and the music a little louder, these guys were the ones that seemed to become the live wires. The girls were more lively than many of the ones I had known. They seemed really content as they swayed to the music. Once in a while, one would get up and start to talk her head off, as if controlled by an outside force . . . I mean, it was weird. Later on, one of the fellows who had asked me to the party came over and suggested I go into the other room with him. Thinking maybe there was some cute chick in there or something, I went along.

It was a cute blonde chick all right, and she sure looked interesting. She was sitting at a table with a burning candle that dimly lit the room. Near the candle were some things lying on the table that did not make sense at first; then, when she raised her arm to light another candle, I noticed she had little bumps on the inside of her arm, with black and blue marks that you could just barely see. Excitement mounted in me, as I realized what the things on the table were for.

She looked me over and motioned for me to sit down. "Would you like to join the rest of the group?" she asked.

"Heroin?" I questioned.

"No," she said, "just speed."

"Sure," I said. "Go ahead and shoot." I rolled up my sleeve and held out my arm. I knew I was tense, but I could not help it. She took hold of my arm and searched for the vein a minute, telling me to make a fist and to relax. As soon as I relaxed, she jabbed the needle in. The expression on her face was something I'll never forget, her eyes almost closed, and her mouth opened. It was as if she had received the fix right along with me. As she pulled the needle out, she smiled deeply and told me to sit there and wait a while.

As I sat there waiting to feel something, I remembered a buddy of mine who had tried "needle speed" and told me of the great feeling of exhilaration and that he had gotten "high" immediately. Then, the next time he had tried it, he had ended up in the hospital with a bad blood infection which took weeks to clear up. At that time a doctor had warned him of all the other dangers he had faced, such as coming down with hepatitis, lockjaw, and the possibility of someone giving him an overdose. The possibility of an overdose should have scared me, but it didn't. Not then. My buddy had told me about someone thay had brought into the hospital when he was there. He had received raw speed and had died moments after the injection. That was enough to stop him—but not me!

I felt great the rest of the evening. By the time I went back to school the next day, I felt like a new person, and I knew that speed was my new bag. I also knew that if I was going to do any more shooting, it would cost me. I was already spending about ten dollars per week on drugs. All the bread I had to depend on was a government grant and social security benefits from the death of my father. I figured it was time I looked around for a part-time job.

Finding the right job was not too easy. I guess my looks scared some people from hiring me. While I must have looked great on the campus, the town itself did not think too much of the way I dressed. I finally found a good part-time job at the California Theater Auto Park. I was one of the "little old men" who take your ticket as you go into the parking lot. It was not a hard job, and I could still be on campus when I wanted to buy drugs.

My popularity grew faster on campus, and my interest in classes began to wane. I started missing more and more classes, just sitting out under the trees and talking with my friends about philosophy and religion and the future of our country. By this time I had gone from a heavyset jovial guy down to 125 pounds. I was neglecting food in favor of drugs and alcohol. Before classes, I had to have something to get me going, something during the day to enable me to stay on top of things, and I depended on downers and booze at night after I returned from my job to get me to sleep.

I finally missed so many classes I was officially classified a drop-out. This put me into a different category now, a campus hanger-on. There were several of us, and we just hung around the student union building all "zacked" up and looking as weird as possible.

I also started pushing drugs. My expenses were going up, and even my part-time job was not enough to support my habit. Dean had introduced me to someone I could get grass from down in National City, south of San Diego, near Tijuana. I would drive down there and pick it up from the "mule." He did not have much trouble getting it from Mexico. I was free to take on as many customers as I could handle, as long as I bought my pot from the same mule.

Dropping away from my old friends was easy, and I did not even bother to go to see my parents. How could I? I was sure Mom would have been able to spot the fact that I was on drugs. She would have raised all kinds of Cain. I also knew she would start quizzing me about school, and I would have to tell her I was a drop-out. My concern for my parents was not enough to stop me from the path I had chosen, but I still had enough sense to stay away from them. I cared about them, but I cared about Mike Warnke more.

I was still looking for something and determined that I

was going to have the best time possible while looking. "If you don't have fun, you're nowhere," was my motto.

One night, in a really rare mood, I closed up the ticket booth early, and let the people park free. There was this party, and I did not want to be late, because the same chick who had introduced me to the needle was going to be there, and she fascinated me. I was afraid if I came in late, I would miss too much of the fun.

The party was great, and I was not sorry I had gone until the next morning. Then I got word that I was fired. I was also accused of stealing some money. It took some fast talking to convince them I had not taken the money—just had not collected it. They did not press charges. They just ended our association by saying, "We can't have anyone working here that we can't trust."

I was pretty put out. I did not know where I was going to get enough money to keep ahead of my habit. It did not occur to me to get a full-time job somewhere. No, I was having too much fun for that.

About a month after I had been fired, I had to start pushing a little harder, as I was running low on money. Things were not going too well, and I guess I showed it. I had to cut down a bit on the drugs in order to afford the necessary dosage. When I went to Dean to get my personal supply, he noticed something was wrong.

"Boy, you're really strung out, you know," he said. "I've been watching you, and I think you have a lot on the ball, but right now you're so dependent on speed that when you don't get it, you're messed up for a bad dog."

"I guess you're right," I said. "But what can I do about it?"

"Well, I know some people, and I know they would be willing to help you. They're squared-away, and they've got the answers. They know where it's at. They're good people, and they take care of their own."

"What could they do for me?" What he had said so far did not make much sense.

"Look, it's not wise to ask too many questions. I know you'll dig this bunch of guys . . . and there will be some good-looking chicks that like to have some real fun, not the kind of freaks that have been hanging around you. These people are into something a whole lot deeper than anything you've been playing around with—like, they will turn you on to a new power without drugs," he said.

"Yeah, yeah," I gulped, hoping I did not sound too anxious. "Why not? You going to pick me up and take me where the action is?"

He nodded and smiled.

Chapter Three

Nineteen sixty-five was a year of new and unsettling events in the world. It was the year of the first spacewalk by the Russians. United States astronauts repeated the performance and chalked up their own firsts with their long flight in orbit and a successful rendezvous. The United States invaded the Dominican Republic and bombed North Vietnam.

Led by Dr. Martin Luther King, blacks marched peacefully in Alabama, but other blacks, stirred up by radicals, rioted in Watts (Los Angeles). A massive power blackout crippled the Northeastern United States and parts of Canada. And for the first time in history, a Catholic pope visited the United States, with New York welcoming Pope Paul VI.

One might see in these events a quickening of the conflict between good and evil, light and darkness, God and Satan.

The year 1965 overall seemed to be a downward turning point for the entire world—for mankind. It was about then that the sale of narcotics suddenly accelerated, the flower children blossomed from out of nowhere, restlessness manifested itself in hundreds of thousands of senseless acts all over the planet, rock music hypnotized, blanked-out thinking, and stirred confused youth to defiance of old values and traditions. Evil seemed to be afoot on Planet Earth.

But if anyone had said anything like that to me, I don't think I could have kept from laughing in his face. I knew it all. I was living in euphoria, and that is not a city in Illinois but a mindless state in which, no matter what I did, only good could happen to me. I was the Wise Man. And everywhere I went, I walked with a perpetual smile.

You see, this guy Dean had come to *me*, had recognized *me* as a superior being who was above all these other mundane cruddy pleasures, someone who could appreciate the special scene he described to me. And he was genuinely concerned about me, because, with all my superior qualities, I was going off the deep end.

The appointed night came. I was picked up and delivered to a really nice home on a hill in the plushest neighborhood of Redlands, California. It was a fantastically beautiful place, high up, with a patio that overlooked the whole city. I could see the lights like a field of softly glowing diamonds. The party guests were around twenty years old. But at first I hardly noticed them; I was gawking at the house—huge rooms, the best furniture, everything gleaming, real oil paintings on the walls, not cheap prints. When I stepped onto that thick carpet, I thought I was off the ground, walking in a cloud. They even had chandeliers, glittering like giant necklaces . . .

This is for me, I thought. This is what I want out of life. When I did take time out to notice the people, there were nineteen or twenty, and they all looked as if they fit the place perfectly, like jewels in a matching setting. Confident faces, good poise, easy talking, clear happy expressions . . . The world's problems were no big thing to them.

And why should I care, anyway, about other people's problems? After all, I reasoned, everyone else was taking care of yours truly—except the weak, misguided, do-gooder spineless ones. After all, what had it gotten me, worrying about them? Just a kick in the pants. "You're not welcome here anymore," the priests had told me, when I mouthed off about the downtrodden.

But these guys and chicks, now, they really had it. They

knew where it was at. And they gave me the nod right away. No questions. A dozen hands stuck out as soon as I walked into that elegant room. Curious but approving eyes swept me up and down, and ready smiles lit their good-looking faces. I was *in* from the start.

We just sat around in a circle and talked and smoked pot. It was not even a ritual. Just hip talk with genuine uninhibited interest in each other. No case histories, no sir! We did not even exchange last names. Dean had cautioned me about that.

As we got higher, the conversation ranged farther out into the twilight zone. Soon the fellows were snuggling up with the girls. And then they split off in couples. It was great, because there was a girl for every guy, not like most places I had been where there is a chronic chick shortage.

Cool-looking, sexy girls, too. And every one was liberal. I mean, *liberal!* These chicks were free-lovers.

As I was saying, they started pairing off in couples, only I do not mean going anywhere. They stayed and did it right there. They were not engaged in just conventional lovemaking, either. They did things that even *I* had not heard about before, nor even dreamed of in an LSD fantasy.

At that time, having this mixed up and basically lonely feeling despite my bravado, I really dug it. It really tipped me out.

"Come on over here, Mike," a blonde said, near the beginning of the whole thing. I could hardly believe it. It couldn't be for real, could it? She initiated one thing after another, bringing others into it, until there wasn't anything I wouldn't do.

Or didn't.

Needless to say, I started attending these parties regularly. And Dean Armstrong, who had introduced me first to drugs, then to the parties, now started subsidizing my drug bill. He was keeping a hard eye on me at these parties. I could have cared less. I was on a sex bender that was greater than any bag I had ever tried before. No sick stomach, no shakes, no flashbacks, no weird freaky feeling

39

of junk between your nerve-ends and your bones. Just soft pink sex—more and more and always enough there to satisfy you.

Gradually, vaguely, I began to notice that at most of the parties, the conversation seemed to drift toward religion. For a while, I wondered what religion had to do with sex. And I came to realize that the kind of religion they were talking about was actual Satan worship. But in the pink haze I was in, that didn't bother me. In fact, it seemed kind of appropriate.

And so they brought me along—patiently, smilingly, bit by bit, taking their time. After a while, Dean began giving me little things to do, like delivering messages or money. It got to the point where almost anything I wanted was mine, as long as I did things for Dean.

"I need a couple of fixes to keep ahead."

"Okay," he would reply. "No sweat." He would hand me a package or bag.

"Oh, while I got you here, there are a couple of things you can do for me. That is, if you have the time."

"My time is your time," I would shrug. Why not? He was feeding me.

"Okay, then. First, tell Ludwig there's a meeting at the barn tomorrow night. Usual time. You know where he lives. He has to use the landlady's phone, and she's a nosey old bat, so we don't like to call. And, hey, while you're in his neighborhood, drop this envelope off at Cliff's. He runs the store on the corner. Uh, wait until there's no customers around."

"You don't have to tell me, Dean."

"Guess not. That's what I like about you, Mike, you're with it."

One time I took some money for a drug payoff down to El Centro, a burg in the desert of California, not far from the border town of Mexicali. A really big load was involved, and this caused quite a flap. It was the most money I had ever seen at one time—$50,000, in bundles of hundred-dollar bills.

One of the messages I carried was an "order" to rough someone up. Another I delivered was hastily scrawled out on the back of a ripped-open package of cigarettes.

I got the idea right away that I was not supposed to know much about what the money was for or what the messages advocated, and that silence was the name of the game, which, if I played it right, earned still more gravy for me.

On the other hand, it was obvious the money was in exchange for narcotics. Often the messages pertained to "meetings," as I discovered despite keeping a cool head and trying not to peek at the messages or ask questions.

Then the time came when Dean deliberately took me into his confidence, to find out just how involved I wanted to get. I told him, "Tuned in and turned on." I never was one to do anything halfway; I was always straining to get over that next hill to see what kind of grass was on the other side.

I quickly pieced together the witchcraft scene, but I was too preoccupied to particularly care. All I saw then was the immediate step ahead for the benefit of yours truly.

One thing did become clear to me, however: this witchcraft thing was *big*—a whole lot bigger than even the most sensational journalism imagined. It wasn't just a kicky fad with people playing "let's pretend." These people were for real, and they played for keeps. When they went after a soul, it was like they were pulling their chairs up to a steak dinner."

When I was finally permitted to attend what they called a "secondary" meeting, I was disappointed. After all the exotic stories I had heard about spells and spirits, summoning demons, hexes, possession, and potions, I was looking for some really subterranean happenings.

But the secondary meetings were pretty mild; in fact, they were much like an ordinary church service, only being a mirror image, with calculated blasphemy the outstanding feature. It dawned on me that the function of the secondary service was to act as a binding together—a fel-

41

lowship or brotherhood type get-together, with a lot of show and socializing, but no honest-to-badness afflicting or even oppressing.

Everyone talked big and gnashed his teeth at Jesus Christ and went through phony rituals that seemed pretty tame and hardly resulted in anyone getting hurt or attacked or anything. But it was a good place to make contacts for dope and get ideas on drumming-up business and trying new gimmicks, yet I always felt the real scene was taken care of somewhere else by secret committees, or a super-organization, or something.

The secondary meetings were, of course, educational, teaching us much witchcraft lore and do-it-yourself formulas which we could try on our own, but they lacked the power and direction I needed to go at it whole hog.

Who were all these people who were being "bound together"? There were several hundred of us, I estimate, spread out in the vast San Bernardino-Riverside-Colton area of Southern California, and many, like myself, had been brought in by way of the sex parties.

The witches were mostly eighteen to thirty years of age, men and women from all walks of life, and I mean *all*: salesmen, carpenters, teachers, students, college professors, housewives, clerks, businessmen, truck drivers, and even a few preachers and priests. We were mostly white and educated, but it was open to all comers, and we had an integrated, ecumenical base that any institution would be proud of.

You could even specialize, like picking a major at college. There were students of Satanism (utilizing the power of the devil through worship); demonology (summoning different demons—the devil's helper); necromancy (communication with the dead by the conjuring up of spirits); vampirism (belief in vampires, blood-sucking ghosts); lycanthropy (assumption of the form and traits of a wolf via witchcraft).

But as I said, I was getting impatient with these secondary meetings, especially as I talked to those in the know who hinted about evil spells, solemn rites, hard-core Satan worship, and really deep stuff. There were quite a few of the higher echelons present, to oversee the "binding together" of the brotherhood of occulists, and they were eyeballing all of us, to see if they could spot any potential leaders.

As I continued carrying messages and proving my reliability with money deliveries, namely, never touching a penny of it, Dean's confidence in me grew. Furthermore, when questioned, I offered intelligent opinions which showed my good judgment and an agile mind. Nor did I pretend I wasn't seeking increased authority; I was perfectly open about it, and at the same time sought every opportunity to submit to my superiors and willingly became more obligated to them. Finally, they decided I was ready, and I was invited to the real thing—a meeting of the *third* stage.

Dean Armstrong behaved mysteriously as we got out of his car that night and walked into a barn located in an orange grove near Redlands.

"You've been a good slave, Mike," he said, pausing at the door. "You've been meeting the population and doing lots of right things for us. So I have a surprise in store for you." He looked at me. "That is, if you want to go along with it."

"I've gone along with everything else," I shrugged.

"All right, I'm going to tell you something." I'd never seen him look so serious.

"I'm a Master Counselor, and my two buddies and I run this group. But we lost a couple of members recently, and we need a replacement who's really with it—someone who will take it seriously. We've been keeping our eyes on you, and we decided you're it. You can join the coven if you want to. But, first, we wanted you to see what it's like. We don't want you to rush into it."

"Let's go."

"Okay," he said, opening the door. "You sit down while I robe up. If you join, you'll get robes, too." He led me to the circle and introduced me to a couple of the guys who were already sitting on the floor around the perimeter of a circle about nine feet in diameter. They were talking when I sat down, so I just listened.

In the center of the circle was the altar—a granite slab supported on two sawhorses. On the slab, a girl lay on her back, nude and waiting, her skin glowing red in the light given off by candles and the balefire burning in a crucible nearby. An inverted cross and an image of a goat's head stood at each end of the altar.

Soon the remainder of the group took their places. Dean and the two other high priests, or counselors, sat on three sides of the altar facing toward the East.

The service was a Black Mass. All the traditional rituals were reversed and deliberately profaned. The sacraments were desecrated. Blasphemies took the place of prayers. Words attributed to Satan were read from the book, *The Great Mother,* which Dean, now standing, held open, resting the back of the book on the girl's stomach.

After the Invocation of Satan, I listened intently to the Offertory, where the members offered their souls to Lord Satan.

I had been high on a massive intravenous jack of speed, excited by the sudden chance to be "in," and in addition, something in the air was going to my head. From having read and talked about rituals, I suddenly realized that the smoke curling up from the crucible on the altar was fumes of deadly nightshade—belladonna. When properly vaporized, it gave off fumes that put you in the right frame of mindlessness. Under all these influences, my mind drifted off.

When the unaccustomed initial effects of the nightshade wore off, I was aware of Dean, who had finished drawing the pentagram on the girl's stomach, saying, "Let those with grievances speak now, that we may all bind together at this hour to direct the power of our father, Satan. As I will, so mote it be."

A guy who had been sitting next to a chick struggled awkwardly to his feet from the floor and stumbled up to the altar. He faced the altar and stretched out his arms.

"There's a guy in Corona, about forty years old. He has

44

a son that got mixed up with speed and then into witch-craft. He's hopping mad about it and is writing all kinds of letters—to congressmen, police officials, the FBI, everybody! He wants a congressional investigation. I think he could be real trouble to us, and we ought to hex him," urged the worshiper.

"You will, then, recite the correct formula for making this plea," Dean commanded. "As I will, so mote it be."

The guy mumbled something. I had a hard time just staying with it, let alone catching his exact words, something about, "Satan, give us this wish, Mr. Joe Somebody, Corona . . ."

The guy next to me got up and tapped me on the shoulder, and I struggled to my feet, tagging after him as he joined the others moving up to surround the petitioner. We circled him, putting our hands on his body and chanting the request to Satan in unison several times.

When we had all resumed our seats, Dean, spreading his arms, faced the pentagram inscribed on the girl's stomach and said, "Master, we petition thee in the name of our Lord Satan to send your messenger to afflict Joe Evans McMillikin. So mote it be!"

I was wide awake, now. This was really where it was at! No more of the phony experimenting. I sat there enthralled, my brain clear and my senses attuned. And then I felt it—the presence. I could almost make out the hazy outline as a demon spirit floated out of that pentagram, and seemed to make a buzzing sound as it dissipated and presumably transferred itself to the locale where it was to do its mischief.

Later, after Dean had changed back to his street clothes —his pin-striped suit and well-creased trousers—metamorphosed again to just an ordinary, everyday guy, I said, "This is for me, man. When can I get initiated?"

We got into the car. "At the next full moon," he said, thoughtfully.

Chapter Four

The next three weeks were murder. Like being without drugs . . . a re-entry . . . withdrawal. Waiting for that full moon was sheer agony. Most guys would have felt mild impatience that leveled off until a day or two before the blast-off, then a frantic few hours of trying to sleep. But not Mike Warnke! I was the guy who could not wait. I wanted what I wanted *now*, with a burning, consuming lust. Tomorrow was forever, today took too long, it should have been yesterday.

It was not the speed I was on that made time a torment. It was just plain Mike! Just me and my demon. I was cross, irritable, and jumpy. I snapped at everyone who talked to me. I had the shakes and flashes. An iron collar compressed the nerves in the back of my neck into hard, tight knots. I was ready to explode.

There was a chick, Louisa, who would stay at my apartment on Pershing Avenue two or three nights a week. I took it out on her; she was my whipping girl. I would not let her go home for almost a week. Then, changing my mind, I kicked her out. "And don't come back," I growled, flinging her bags after her as she stumbled blindly down the stairs and out onto the street.

I had the impulse to throw down some empty wine bottles along with her bags, but then my eye caught a nearly full bottle, and it seemed more interesting to empty it.

I was on temporary layoff from my new part-time job at

a hamburger stand, so the days seemed even longer. Dean was not helping me pass the time, either. He seemed to have suddenly run out of errands for me to do. He did not communicate with me during the entire time. This added to my anxiety. What was going on? I drew a blank every time I tried to get in touch with him. He did not like anyone trying to contact him. It was on an *"I'll* call *you"* basis. But I was desperate . . . and unsuccessful.

He had given me a good supply of reds and speed just before making his proposition, but I used that up in record time. When I was out and in a panic, the guy I called trying to locate Dean said he would be glad to send over enough to tide me over, which he did. He also reminded me that the big meeting was only two days off. Two more days of torment.

I stared holes in the calendar. It was one put out by an Aquarius-oriented printer with all the astrological claptrap mixed with genuine astronomical data, including the phases of the moon illustrated and drawn to look like a man with eyes, nose, and mouth—a grinning mouth, sneering at me.

One night when I was drunk, I stood outside in the little backyard of the apartments and glared up at the moon. It certainly looked full enough, as it does for a few days before and after it is officially "full." The crater shadows made it look like a man's face, and I snarled, shaking my fist at him.

The apartment superintendent came out just then to move the garbage cans to the alley for tomorrow's collection. He stood with his hand on a lid, observing me. "You need to relax, Mike," he said softly. "Why don't you come up to my apartment and have a drink?"

"I was just going up to go to bed," I replied not wanting anything to do with that fag. "Just practicing some lines I have to do for a play at college. I'm supposed to be a werewolf."

"Happy howling, then, Mikie," he replied, lifting the can onto a dolly and wheeling it toward the gate.

The next morning, I made my appearance on campus to

dispense a little knowledge, but my crowd of listeners, freshmen mostly, who usually appreciated me putting them straight on the Establishment, drifted away when I growled every time one of them dared voice a question. I was soon sitting under the tree talking to myself.

When the evening of the meeting finally did arrive, the phone rang and Dean said, "I just wanted to remind you . . ."

I got kind of hot and huffy, though I did not let him know it. All those weeks, while I was cooling my heels and not hearing a peep from him, I had been suppressing the fear that he had changed his mind, or it was all a dirty trick to make me go ape, or something. Now he blithely calls and reminds me to be on time.

I got into my car and started out, erratically tooling the vehicle out of town and down a country road, along the orange groves, toward that one particular grove. Ominous clouds hung in the sky, and the only indication of the moon was a sheet of blue-white filtering through a massive cloud bank nearly overhead. I peered out, trying to locate the turnoff in the light cast by the headlights and almost missed it.

I parked in the darkness by the side of the road and got out and stood by the car a minute in the gloom, suddenly almost afraid. Dark and tall, sprawling trees, looking like black giants—trees used by growers as windbreaks for the shorter orange trees—hovered round me and made it even darker. The clouds had thickened, and the night air was humid and oppressive and charged with electricity. It was one of those threatening summer storms that, in Southern California at that time of year, seldom materialize.

I slammed the door of the car to show I was not afraid and hurried to the barn, which was a large black square in the night, set back off the road. As I got closer, I could see other cars parked in the concealment of trees, tall weeds, and scraggly bushes. I knew I had goofed and should have parked my car out of sight like the others had. I hesitated, wondering whether to go back, when I saw coming out of

48

the barn a tall, slim man dressed in a business suit, who was illuminated by the moon shining through a momentary gap in the clouds.

I did not recognize him as one of the brothers, and I got on the defensive, saying, "What are you doing here?"

He patted me on the head with a spade-like hand at the end of his long arm, as though I was a dog, and said, "That's all right. I was just talking with your leader. *We*— I—had a request, and Dean agreed to bring it up during the meeting."

He sauntered off toward where the cars were parked, and I shivered. Something about him—something about his bearing, his patronizing superiority, his overflowing self-confidence, all this laced with lurking evil—unnerved me. And also aroused my envy.

I habitually projected this cocky demeanor, and I put it across okay on dumb punks, but this guy was really *it*. I looked upon him as a threat, a challenge, a rival—a rival possessing ability that might be hard for me to match.

Dean was just inside the door when I went in. He was robed and ready.

"I just saw a guy snooping around outside," I muttered. "A real creep. He seemed to know about us . . ."

"Easy, man, about who you call a creep. He could be a brother. A *big* brother." Dean took my arm and guided me toward the interior of the barn.

"He said he was talking to you."

Dean tightened his grip on my arm. "If he said so, he must be right. You don't question those guys. Right now, you think our group is top drawer. You keep thinking that way and have pride in your outfit. But, remember this; there could be something even bigger than us." He led me to where the group was scattered in small groups talking in low tones.

With a ceremonious gesture and incantation, after bowing to the East, Dean swept up the sword, said a blessing, then walked around the altar, trailing the point of the sword on the rough-hewn wooden floor, on which you could see the marks of a dozen other circles where swords had pricked up bits of the wood. Someone followed behind him with chalk.

One of the brothers lit the candles and Dean signaled someone else to switch off the light. The brothers took their places on the perimeter of the circle, facing in, and Dean turned to me. "Strip," he hissed.

I glanced around at the guys and chicks, and for the first time, their eyes, in the candle and crucible-fire, seemed narrow and mean.

"Sure," I said, clearing my throat. I untied my thin purple tie, unbuttoned and removed my orange shirt with the large blue polka dots, unbuckled my belt, and let my pants fall to the floor. I wasn't worried about my dry-cleaning bill just then.

When I was completely naked, I was told to kneel, facing the altar. "Take this necklace," Dean murmured, "and hold it in your left hand."

Dean extended both arms out in front of him, toward the altar, so that the sleeves of his robe hung down from his forearms. He pivoted to face the East and said, "Lord Master Satan, the high priests of this, your coven, have agreed to accept a new brother into this unholy congregation, and we pray for your blessing and approval."

The other members made a chant and clapped their hands.

"Power of Darkness," Dean went on, his arms still raised and his face grim, "let us have a sign that you will accept Mike, to be called Judas, into the brotherhood of your slaves." Dean closed his eyes, meditated, and time seemed to crawl.

I was so shaky I could hardly maintain my kneeling position. I felt like I was going to pitch forward on my face. My knees ached. It was a warm evening so I was not cold, yet I felt icy, as if my blood, or something else, had drained out of me. Then, too, I was up closer to the burner in which was smoldering the substance that gave out the nightshade fumes. I could tell that in another crucible, some pot had been mixed with the perfumed

50

material that was billowing out of the burner. In a third, sulphur was sputtering out the acrid odor of sulphur dioxide, the smoke laced with edges of blue fire. I felt my aching knees wobble under me.

Suddenly, Dean gave a loud, piercing moan. A sardonic grin consumed the lower part of his face. "Thank you, Lord of Darkness," he said, almost in ecstasy, "for your favorable reply." He looked down at me. "Rise, Judas Iscariot, and prepare to dedicate your soul to our Lord Satan."

I got to my feet.

"Hood," he pronounced, and one of the other two counselors, the Keeper of the Seal, handed him the hood. It was similar to the headgear of the Eastern Orthodox religion, like that worn by Archbishop Makarios, resembling an Egyptian headdress raised high on the head.

Dean wafted the hood over the fumes from the burners, then dipped his fingers in a chalice of holy water, which I later learned was water in which the priests had urinated. He sprinkled the hood with the water and said, "Master of Darkness and demons, to thee we dedicate this hood for the use of your slave and our new brother for his servicie to thee."

He placed the hood on my head, then turned to the Keeper of the Seal and nodded, whereupon the counselor handed him the black, long-sleeved inner robe. Dean performed a similar gesture and incantation and helped me put this robe on. He repeated this procedure and helped me on with the black, sleeveless outer robe, which was like a floor-length vest. He pushed me back a few paces from the altar and made some passes over me as he said, "You are now robed for he service of Satan. Now, unclench your hand and let us dedicate the necklace you will wear."

On the end of the necklace was my amulet, a three-inch-long pendant with an elongated silver scorpion, my zodiac sign. He dipped the pendant briefly into each burner in turn, enough for it to be surrounded by smoke, then dipped it quickly in the chalice of urine-desecrated holy water. He shook it so some of the drops splattered on my

51

bare feet. Then, when I had bent my head forward in response to his gesture, he slipped the chain around my neck, tucking it under the collar of the inner robe.

Dean turned to the Keeper of the Seal, his brother priest, and said, "Ring!" He was handed a large, silver ring which carried the symbol of left hand, palm forward, with a pentagram and crescent in the hand's center.

"This ring," he said, "that is dedicated to our master, you shall wear only when you meet with others to do the business of Satan, or bless his name, or ask his help. You shall keep this ring safe from harm in a dark hiding place, except when you congregate to do Satan's bidding. No one else is to wear this ring, or the demon guarding it will destroy you both."

Nodding, I extended my left index finger, and he, with great solemnnity, made ready to slide the ring on my finger. "Before sealing this initiation ceremony with the placing of the ring, you, Judas, are now to confess your dedication to Satan, offering his Lordship your soul. So mote it be."

He cleared his throat and continued, "Repeat after me: I, known here as Judas, do hereby and now, forever and a day, submit my soul to the custody and care of his Highness of Darkness, Satan, Master of the World."

He started over more slowly and had me repeat each phrase after him. Then he slid the ring on my finger.

The chill I had been feeling up to that point, even after the robes had been laid upon by body, suddenly vanished, and in its place, fire seemed to flood through me. My mouth went dry, and I sensed a thin wisp of vapor flow from my mouth and nose. Now I was burning—consumed with hell's flame, my heart racing and my pulses pounding. It was an ecstatic fever that caused perspiration to stream from my pores. I felt light on my feet, floating.

Yet, even at this moment, the son of Whitey Warnke narrowed his eyes as he caught a glimpse of the ring on Dean Armstrong's left index finger. It was similar to the one I had just received, yet embellished with a more elaborate floral design around the palm and bearing a mystic symbol, showing the special status and focus of power which only Master Counselors can have.

I thought, even at this high point, "I will be wearing a ring like that—soon."

It was the same old thing: always wanting to be big. No sooner scaling one mountain peak than having my eyes on an even higher pinnacle.

I was jolted out of my reverie by the awareness that Dean was repeating something he had obviously just said but which I had not heard.

"The Book," he called, as he picked up the knife which had been dedicated earlier. "Hold out your right wrist."

I looked at the knife and then my wrist. What was this? I wondered.

He found a place near an artery and made an incision there. I jerked violently in pain, but he held my arm tightly with his other hand; he caught the blood in an eye-cup and thrust a handkerchief at me to stop the flow. It had happened so fast that I had not had time to realize what was going on.

"Now, dip this quill in the blood and sign your new name." He handed me the feather pen and shoved the book at me, a large, black, leather-bound book two-feet square and almost a foot thick. He held it for me, open near the middle. The yellow-edged pages showed three columns each, the left side full of names and the right about half-used. All the names were written in blood which had dried and darkened and looked black in the illumination in the barn—except for one name which reflected a greenish tone.

"What's with the *green* bit?" I whispered, as I shakily began to scrawl my name. I wanted to know, like, *now*.

"That's if you cop out," Dean whispered. "It does that. Don't ask me how. If someone unlocks the book and opens it and sees one of the signatures *green*, he knows that guy copped out. There aren't too many. It's not healthy to cop out. Satan doesn't like to admit he lost a soul. When he doesn't like something, it makes him mad. And when he gets mad, you've had it. It's not too healthy to have your name turn green."

Well, I had just dedicated my soul to Satan. Thinking about it and the Book of Names and the green ink made me suddenly realize the enormity of what I had done. I licked my lips.

For the next few days, Dean made up for not having given me anything to do to earn my drugs. Even though I had been called back to work at my four-hour-a-day afternoon job as a cook in a hamburger stand, I might have been totally unemployed as far as Dean was concerned. Besides, I still spent several hours each morning on the campus of San Bernardino Valley College, reading under my eucalyptus tree or holding my grassy conferences with guys and chicks, making little deals, or browsing in the library picking up whatever knowledge I could, as well as attracting the attention that meant so much to me. It was a habit hard to break, and most of Dean's errands came during the hours of darkness, which meant that mainly my sleep was what suffered. I just took more speed to keep up with the race.

Also, I intensified my studies of witchcraft and magic. If I was going to get to the top of the organization—and it was strongly hinted that the job of Master Counselor led on to still higher goals, toward which Dean was striving— I had to know my subject backward and forward—especially backward, like reciting familiar prayers backward.

One of the members of the coven, a thirty-five-year-old trim redhead named Teresa, seemed to be just the one to help me find some shortcuts. She appeared willing enough to share her knowledge and experiences, so, one night, after one of the meetings, I asked her if we could get together and compare notes. "Sure," she said. "Anytime."

"Your place or mine?" I asked, grinning.

She gave me a strange look and said, "If you have time right now, come on over; there's no time like the present. I live on Fern Street. Just follow my car."

I trailed her out of the parking area in the bushes near the barn, and kept close enough so the headlights on my car formed a kind of link between us. As I drove—too slowly for my taste—I pondered in my mind what to make of Teresa. Her crisp, serious tone of voice baffled me, and I could not tell whether she was on the defensive about being attracted to a younger guy, or was deliberately and definitely trying to say that this was strictly an educational affair.

When I got to her apartment, she sat in a chair almost across the room from me and said, "Mike, we can enjoy ourselves, our fellowship, and share good times together, but remember this: you've gotten youself into a serious business. It's not a matter of fun-and-games during the meetings, not like those first-stage orgies and second-stage sophomoric horsing-around sessions. Our Brotherhood means business, and our rituals are serious."

I laughed a little nervously. "I know. I know."

"Well, I noticed you looking around and snickering . . ."

I shrugged. "Listen, I've been studying witchcraft and the occult for a long time."

"But you have to remember that any levity or disrespect during the actual ceremonies is liable to have demons down on our necks. Everything's *got* to be done properly. After the meetings, if some gal and guy want to goof off or get together with a whole group of others, that's okay. That's your reward. As for me, I haven't time."

"Yeah. Well, I got the idea you're a pretty busy girl, Teresa, and I hope I'm not taking up your valuable time . . ."

"When it comes to steering a brother in the right direction, I have all the time in the world," she said. "Now. You mentioned one night that you had read a great deal about potions but hadn't really seen any mixed up or used."

"Yeah," I replied. "I mean, like, I wonder if they are still really used by serious witches and if, well, if they're for real. You know."

"There's no time like the present, Mike, to extend your knowledge and see for yourself." She got up and went to a sideboard which was packed inside with witchcraft items. In appearance, her apartment gave not the slightest hint of her occult involvement, but her cupboards and closets had it all there, the whole outlay. She had a good number of straight friends who would come in to visit, and she had a perfect front. Would they have been shocked if they had seen what was stashed around the apartment!

She hauled out a regular, old, stained mortar and pestle and several vials and jars, some with liquid, some with powder or bits of herbs. She glanced at the large clock with silver Roman numerals above the sideboard.

"The stuff I'll mix, when vaporized, will carry your wish, and it will be done before daylight." She lit a couple of gold candles and switched off the lights. She was breathing heavily, and the perfume she wore mingled with the smoke from the scented candles.

I was very careful not to betray any sign of disbelief, but I could not help thinking this was too much. She lined up the vials beside the mixing bowl and then, moving slowly and precisely, used a graduated spoon to measure out a small bit from each container. She ground the solids together, then added the liquids and stirred them with an iron rod. When it was all mixed up, it was the consistency of a thick paste. She scooped some of it into a spoon and then glanced again at the clock.

"Maybe if I sprinkled a little pot on the spoon," I suggested, "it would magnify the effects." I reached into my pocket.

She gave me that strange look again, and I dropped my poke. "It could be disastrous," she replied in a low tone. "Why do you think I keep glancing at the clock? There are only certain minutes when you can vaporize it properly. The time has to be exactly right. The ingredients. The place. The way you do it, the silver spoon, the containers, the incantations I'm going to pronounce. Everything has to be as prescribed by the formula. There are many other things we could have mixed up tonight, but the time is not right. I chose *wishing smoke*, because the time, place, and planets are all right for it. Change any one element—the day, the ingredient, the amount of any one item—and you don't know what the hell will open up. See this scar?" She pointed to a bluish stitch-like line just in front of her ear. I nodded.

"An enraged demon clawed me there. They don't like to have to obey you, and if you give them the smallest excuse, they'll turn on you. They're like mad dogs. I couldn't see him, but I felt it, that's for sure." She lapsed into quiet, then intoned something in Latin.

She was really way out. And I was a little shook and kept my mouth shut.

Suddenly, she inhaled sharply. "Now!" She grabbed up the spoon and held it over the burner. A thin greenish vapor uncurled. She recited something else in Hebrew, then shouted, "Now, make your request known!"

Part of me just couldn't believe it was really happening —I mean, a sophisticated, suburban-type American woman with a neat red bob, wearing a trim gray-skirted suit, acting weird over an alchemy apparatus. In my musing, I had not gotten around to deciding upon a wish, so I was startled into an instant decision and thought, "I wish Teresa would fall at my feet and beg me to make love to her." I strained to keep from chuckling at the whole thing and also at the spontaneous wish which had caught even me by surprise. I was glad I had not said it aloud.

The next second I was staring in fascination as Teresa abruptly dropped the spoon, gazed up at me, her shoulders hunched slightly forward.

She shook her head as though trying to throw off an unwelcome compulsion. She stepped back slowly from me, saying, "No, no," knocking into the table which contained the apparatus. She swallowed a lump in her throat and bit her lip, struggling with unseen forces.

I was scared to death.

Then she sighed deeply and sharply and started muttering. "I know what you wish. Why did you do it? I told you, this isn't a game anymore." She gave up resisting and dropped to her feet and kissed my ankles.

I was stunned. Serious now, I bent over and put a hand on her arm and coaxed her up. "No! I'm sorry. I guess I still wasn't really convinced. I didn't really mean it. I just couldn't think of anything else on the spur of the moment. I didn't want this to happen, really. You're too with-it. Besides—" I gulped, glancing at the witchcraft paraphernalia on the table and shuddering, "when it was over, and you came out of it, you might be mad and—Don't hold it against me, all right?"

She looked at me calmly. "I won't hold it against you, Mike. You just didn't know. You still didn't believe. You do now."

I nodded. I felt weak in the knees. It was hard to believe, but I believed now.

At that moment, seeing Teresa compose herself and revert back to the serious and businesslike servant of Satan which she was in her normal state, I believed in Satan's powers fully—and I wanted to control them.

When I got home, I glanced at the small alarm clock on my bedside table. For once, I was home at a reasonable hour. It was only eleven o'clock. I got ready for bed and sat up in bed to have a glass of wine and flip through a magazine.

There was a light rapping on the door. I opened it cautiously. It was Dean. He seldom came in person. I was curious. I let him in and bolted the door.

"In the sack already?" he inquired, sitting in a chair as I sat on the horsehair sofa in the living room. "Man, you ought to be out hustling . . ."

I gulped. "Now, there's one thing I draw the line on—"

"You want to make it to the top, don't you, Mike? You've got to *work*."

He snorted. "You've got a slick tongue, Mike. Our master expects you to put your best foot forward and use your abilities up to their limits. And beyond. A guy like you, now, could really go out and swing and bring in the crowd. You're holding back on Satan, Mike. Coasting."

I shrugged. "I talk to kids at the college almost every day. Push my share of the stuff and split the profit with you. Of course, I feel like I have to be careful what I say and size them up and all that. You, yourself, told me—"

He waved his hand. "But there are ways and there are ways, Mike. It has to be done on an organized, systematic, planned basis. Take right now. You could be out on the strip, getting acquainted with guys at the bars, doing a little hard-core recruiting. After all, I had Bill fix you up with a fake ID card showing you're over twenty-one. Haven't you ever heard of Melanie? She'll work with you."

"I don't understand," I said.

"Well, we've got to get the guys and chicks started with the parties, first, where we can give them an eyeballing. Right? The first-stage. Get them involved. To the hilt. Then, after giving them a good look, pick out a few for second-stage. The best prospects, and the ones who are ready."

"Roger. But, how does Melanie fit in?"

"You haven't heard of her, then? Well, after you screen a guy, you take him up to her apartment. Then act as her foil. Let her do the work. But, you've got to make the contacts first. Screen out the squares. Soften up the marks, provide the readiness."

"It boils down to getting them gradually involved, leading up to the drug and witchcraft bit by easy stages." I understood what he was getting at.

"A lot of them will be dopeheads already. But you tell them you know some guys who can put them on some really first-class stuff. Melanie is available day and night. You start with the dope and the sex. Just contact her a few hours ahead of time to see if she's got anything planned or if someone else is already coming up to her pad."

"Well, I'll get to the campus early and give it a whirl. Then call her."

"Good show. Only, there's still time tonight to see what you can do. I'd suggest Bluebeard's. That's where all the guys go who just recently turned twenty-one. They're out for a real binge, and they're a good bet."

Dean called Melanie from my apartment and introduced us on the phone before he left. "Your coven name is Judas?" Melanie asked.

"Yeah. I'll see you later. Tonight, if I'm successful," I answered.

Bluebeard's was both half-lit and half-filled. The patrons were also half-lit. They were mostly young punks, with a few chicks scattered along the bar. I spotted a guy I knew from the college, and the seats on either side of him being occupied, I pushed my way in and stood beside him.

Claude was writing a term paper on sexual fantasies. During talks with him on the campus, I had learned he was having a rough time because he just could not push himself forward enough with the girls. His sharp, blemished features did not help any.

"I got some more material for your term paper in psychology," I said, after the formalities. "Like, man, they did this study about how much sex a guy *really* needs and how much he can really perform if he has a chance and the right partner, and all that."

We had a few drinks as we discussed the subject. It was getting close to closing time and we were shoving the drinks down fast. He wanted to make an A on the paper to balance a couple of D's and come out with straight C's for his postsummer session.

"Actually," I said, "I know a nympho who's real flipped on the subject herself and is willing to be a 'living laboratory.' In fact, I was going to see her just after two, on my way home, and she said I could bring a friend if I wanted to. My idea was to look at some drawings she did that I might want to hang in my pad, but, knowing Melanie, she could be persuaded to do a little experimenting." I shrugged. "However, you're obviously too tired. Have to get up and get to that class. Maybe some other time . . ."

"Well, it *is* kind of sudden, though I'm not all that tired."

"Ah, but this late at night, and with all that liquor you

put down, you couldn't do her justice. Not a nympho like Melanie . . ."

"Bet me!" he snorted, almost angry. "It's just having the opportunity that's been my problem, that's all." His adam's apple bobbed. "The right chance and the right girl." He banged his fist on the bar.

"Well," I said, sounding full of compassion, "maybe you'd better come along with me after all and give it a try."

Expecting me to deliver despite the doubts I'd expressed on the phone, Melanie had prepared a nice little supper for us and took it out of the refrigerator after letting us in. "I knew you'd be successful, Mike—" she said when I went into the kitchenette by myself—"with that slick mouth I've heard so much about."

I had not had a date with Melanie, though I had seen her when I was still in the second-stage. She did not need to go up the ladder any. She did very well on her particular rung. She was shapely, sensuous, and had long dark hair and fluttering brown eyes. "You know, I really *am* a nympho," she whispered as we started out of the kitchenette.

Claude was really impressed. Melanie sat next to him on the sofa, and before long she had him very interested. She asked him to try a new dance step, as an excuse to get him real close, a real slow number, and before I knew it, they were in the bedroom while I stretched out on the sofa to get what I wanted most, a few minutes of good plain sleep.

We left later, and on the way, I told Claude that Melanie had said she liked him and that she hoped I would bring him over again sometime.

I had had to play all this by ear. The next morning, before I left my apartment for my informal seminar at my tree of higher learning, I called Melanie, waking her up, and had a long talk about future encounters. She said she had assumed that I knew the "system" and that I should do pretty much what I had done—act as an innocent third party. She said to bring Claude over a couple more times for sex.

"On the third visit, I'll pretend that you two were unexpected," she continued. "I'll be in my witch's robe and tell you guys I was just about to cast a spell. I have several good routines that always impress the guys. So, Mike, you act real surprised. Real dumb. Say something like, 'Holy cow! *A witch?*'"

The way she put it, she was using psychology on *me*, making me feel how important I was in the plan, appealing to my flair for the dramatic, challenging my acting ability, appealing to my ego, my imagination, making me feel confident. I was a partner in a plot to get people involved in first-stage parties, from whence the road for the initiate would lead toward the second-stage and, perhaps, the finale, the third-stage.

The people we wanted had to be vaguely dissatisfied with their environment and experiences, had to have a certain amount of guts, yet have some weakness and perhaps even some fear.

But if they did not have fear, then they had to be completely devoid of a moral conscience. Like me, then. They also had to have a peculiar kind of instability which made them ripe for dope and witchcraft and the crimes that went along with it.

The kind of guy who was the best candidate for all of this was not always easy to get to. He was usually suspicious. He thought he knew the score, even if he did not. He usually put on a front of having seen it all and being very skeptical that you could show him anything that would turn him on. Most of them were either on a low level of drugs or would be if you worked it right. Also, if they did not have bundles of money, it was great, because we could use money along with sex to grab them in. If they had plenty of bread, we could offer them power and sex. If they already had both money and power, we could still offer them sex. Sex had the most facets.

For all these reasons, you could not just go up to a guy

and say, "Hi! Would you like some sex tonight?" Then, later, "Now that you've gotten your kicks with Melanie, how about trying the drug scene? And make yourself some loot to boot?" And, still later, "Bored? We got something else in our Pandora's box. Ever think about being a witch?" No. It was not as cut and dried as all this. We had to pick our candidates carefully and lead carefully and purposefully from one step to the next.

So it was the end of the week before I was ready to introduce Claude to the witch trip at Melanie's place. On his third visit, he was ripe to be sucked in.

When we arrived at Melanie's, I affected a pose and said, *"You're a witch?"* after she had pretended surprise at our appearance and mentioned she was about to cast a spell. "You're putting me on!"

"No, Mike, honestly," Melanie protested. "You believe me, don't you, Claude, honey?" She looked at him with those seductive eyes wide in innocence.

"I'd believe anything about you, baby," he said.

But then she asked if one of us would like to be her guinea pig, and he sobered, a taint of suspiciousness still clinging.

"No sweat," I said, stepping forward. "I'll be 'it.' I'm no chicken."

Claude said, "Now, wait. Let me reconsider." He thought about the angles and decided he could be more sure it was for real if he was personally involved. It worked like a charm, and he was impressed, especially after she let her robe slide to the floor and stood before him naked. He was really grabbed in.

Claude was a perfect setup, now, for those first-stage full-blown sex orgies laced with a taste of witchcraft. Melanie had enticed from him his latent sexual lust and made him feel his sexual resources were unlimited.

I lost track of him after that because someone else carried the ball from that point. If he was with-it, though, I would see him later, at his initiation into the third-stage.

And that was the way it was done. That method was

duplicated hundreds of times during the following months by myself and my cohorts using a number of different chicks.

For the next several weeks, Dean didn't keep his promise about cutting down on the monotonous deliveries.

"We just have too much business right now and not enough guys yet, to do it all," he explained. "When the ones you've been getting for us get more involved—we can't just shove them into it the first week or two—they can start taking over more of this drug stuff." He paused, winking, and then continued, offhandedly, "I've been noticing you've been asking for a lot more speed and downers yourself lately, among other things . . ."

Well, I was putting in about twenty hours a day, divided between my part-time job which I kept as a front, recruiting people for witchcraft, making deliveries, and running other errands. It was beginning to get to me.

I was *really* ticked off when at 3:00 A.M. a couple of days later, I was awakened by a low but persistent "pssst" in my ear. I warily opened my eyes. Then I recognized Dean, standing by the head of my bed. "How'd you get in?" I yawned. "The door was bolted."

"Never mind that," he answered in a thin voice. The night light, which I had installed because of bad dreams, made him look pasty.

"Let me guess: you want me to take a bunch of grass somewhere. Probably to San Diego. And manicure it, too."

"No, no," Dean said, shaking his head. "I just came back from a long conference with some big people, and my schedule for tomorrow is like impossible, so I won't have time for even a phone call. Anyway, as Teresa says, 'There's no time like the present.'"

"Even if it's two or three in the morning," I muttered.

"So, get this: I'm being moved up. Way up. You got to take my place, Mike."

Take his place. Just like that. No preliminaries. When they decided something, it was as good as done. It was the chance I had been waiting and working for. And it was thrown at me like you would throw some leftover meat to the dog. "Sure," I said weakly. I yawned a couple of times and then gathered enough calm and waking up enough to ask, "What's up?"

"It's better I don't come out and name it," he said. "But they, the big guys, like my style and want me up on their level. I've got an assignment in Mississippi. A real challenge."

Mississippi! Were we pawns on a giant chessboard? I wondered. Who was playing this game?

"First off, I spend a week or two at a training conference up North. Then I go to work. Meanwhile, you dig in and study the ritual backward and forward. Rehearse so you can get the right tone of voice in it and do it in your sleep without shaking or stuttering—high or low, under any conditions. Practice and then practice some more. Get a bunch of guys and chicks together to help you. You get initiated tomorrow night. Actually, that's tonight if you want to be technical. Then, after that, you have a week before you actually take over a meeting. Make that week count. Remember, from here out, whatever you want is yours. Name it. The Brotherhood will zap it to you. Rent? Forget it. We might even give you an extra apartment. Food? Just give the Keeper of the Seal a weekly shopping list and list of places you want to dine out on given nights. Transportation? No sweat. You know where you can charge the gas. You've got a free ticket.

"And, Mike—" He smiled for the first time. "You don't got to make no more deliveries, I reckon." He must have started practicing his drawl for Mississippi.

It was too good to be true. I thought maybe it was all a dream, but in the morning there were signs that he had been present—an empty glass in which he had poured himself some cognac, cigarette butts, and a number scrawled on a scratch pad as a talisman of the occasion.

I did as directed, and I called up several friends from the coven and told them what was happening. I told them if they wanted to be "in" with the *new* counselor, they had jolly well better help me with my lines.

I knew even before initiation tonight that for the coming week and weeks after that, I would be drifting on a cloud of euphoria.

I, Mike Warnke, was to be one of the three Master Counselors—high priests—of the Brotherhood. I would have all the booze I could drink, all the broads I wanted, and life-or-death control, literally, over a whole legion of people.

I was under a spell.

Chapter Five

The night of the full moon turned out to be beautiful with the moonshine creating a golden yellow glow on the hillsides. I stood looking out the window of my apartment, watching that moon. Dean would be by to pick me up soon. This was the night I was to become a high priest—a Master Counselor. So mote it be.

As I stood there looking out of the window, a sleek black Lincoln Continental pulled up. Dean got out and looked up to see if I was ready. I waved and nodded, then locked the door on the way out and bounded down the stairs.

Dean kind of laughed when I leaped into the car and slammed the door. "Slow down, boy, and try to gain a little more composure. You're going to need it. Remember, this is a serious ceremony, and all you have been learning in the past few weeks is going to come in handy."

"Yeah. I know," I replied, trying not to show any nervousness in my voice. "I stayed up half the night just studying this ceremony one last time. I'm not too clear about some of the other ones yet. But I have a week to bone up."

Dean looked over at me, as if studying me closely for the first time. "You'll do all right, buddy. You've got a good mind. I've seen the way you go about learning something when you want to. You already know that this ceremony will be outside in a field, back of the barn. I'm not sure anyone told you about the power of the ring you'll be receiving tonight. I know there will be great emphasis put on it, but someone might have forgotten to tell you that this power could be used against you, for instance, if you should decide to flake off with the ring. We only wear them during our rituals. By the way, what sign are you wearing now?"

"Capricorn," I replied, "to give me the wisdom to conduct these meetings the way they should be."

We were out in the country, now, the moon casting shadows of the trees that lined the road. When we drove up by the trees that had threatened me before, I gave them the finger. This time I was arriving in style, a style that I hoped would soon become mine.

We sighted the barn, and Dean drove around to the back, following a small road I had not seen before. He drove back into the trees before stopping, then turned around to make sure the car was hidden.

When we arrived at the ceremony site, the altar was in place. There were a few people milling about. As we came up to the circle, Dean introduced me to some members I had not seen before. They were taking the place of a couple who had gone on to another group or something, according to Dean.

"This will be your new Master Counselor after tonight," he told them, and I had a hard time not swelling up inside my body. They gave me the special handshake with the little and index fingers extended.

"Time to robe up," Dean said. "Looks like we'll have our share of people tonight." He was looking toward the hidden parking lot, and I noticed there were still more cars coming in. "Hey, Andy, keep that fire down. We need attention like we need holes in our heads."

As soon as we were in our robes, as if by a pre-arranged signal, the girl came out of the bushes. The moonlight made her look pale, and I suspect she was also a little chilly, though she looked as if she was in a trance and would not have minded if it was thirty-two degrees.

She was tall and statuesque and walked with grace toward the altar. Her skin had a slight shine, as if she had rubbed some oil into it. Many eyes followed her as she arranged herself on the altar. It was difficult to concentrate on the beginning of the ceremony at first, looking at this beautiful chick with the firelight and moonlight playing tricks on her skin.

Dean was exorcizing the knives, getting them ready to be used later. He was also dedicating everything in sight, and now I understood what the chants meant.

As the chanting began, we were all sitting on the ground in a circle. I looked over at the goat's head and the Great Mother on a stand with two candles beside it. Suddenly, I spotted the ring beside one of the candles. It caught the light of the fire and shone as if beckoning to me. It was silver, and I could recall the design, the outstretched palm with the crescent and star in it, the sculptured vine around the perimeter. This was the ring I had wanted for my finger, the one that was a little more elaborate than the one the others wore.

Dean went to the altar and picked up the ring. "Judas, come forward." While I got up, he went to the fire and passed the ring through it once, saying, "Fire of Art, cleanse away all evil and malice toward our brother Judas adhering to this ring."

Then he turned and put it into a bowl of water, saying, "Water of Purity, cleanse away all evil adhering to this ring." The ring was held up for all to see. It gleamed in the candlelight, and I could see the power coming from it. Dean turned and placed the ring on my finger.

I repeated back to him, "Ring of Art, blessed be, focus of power to thee. The wearer be blessed as all the rest, and as I will, so mote it be."

"Judas is your new counselor, Master of Rituals," Dean intoned. "And the well-being of all of you depends upon his well-being. Treat him with reverence and respect and come to him with any problems that you may have regarding ritual. He will be your go-between from now on.

He has studied hard and wishes to serve Satan." Then Dean motioned for me to sit down, and I walked in a daze back to my place.

Was that really me, Mike Warnke, up there? The fire was getting warmer, and my excitement was so great, I could not even follow the rest of the service.

Afterward, we were all invited to this chick's place up in the hills, another one of those exclusive homes with the large glassed-in areas. This place had a garden pool in the center and a skylight ceiling that was partly open to the stars. Tiki torches lighted the pool area, and large tropical plants were scattered around. There was plank decking all around the pool. Small white iron tables with individual candles were grouped in intimate settings. Our drinks were served by a small man in a white dinner jacket, and two girls kept bringing in trays of hot canapés with things like anchovies, chicken livers on toothpicks, small rolled turkey sandwiches, and a bunch of other goodies I could only guess at.

Liquor flowed plentifully, and this time almost everyone was dressed as though they were at a swank cocktail party. I had followed Dean's advice and toned my clothing down a little, and I could see why, after looking around at the people. The chick that gave the party was up in the "social set," and she did not want a bunch of weird guys hanging around the place to attract attention.

I was beginning to come out of my state of euphoria, and when I realized the party was in my honor, I really outdid myself. I hobnobbed with the people that Dean introduced me to during the party. My new status was already upon my shoulders.

"Say, Mike, how about us getting together and going over any new thoughts you might have on the rituals? With two of us coming in new as counselors, it's a good time to sweep away some cobwebs," Andy suggested. He was about my age and had already been initiated as Keeper of the Books, a month earlier. At the next meeting, we were to initiate still another counselor, the new

Keeper of the Seal. It seemed that there was suddenly a big acceleration in the turnover. I did not know what had happened to cause a vacancy in the office of the Keeper of the Seal, but Andy was replacing someone who had just dropped out of sight—a guy who had started letting his conscience get in his way. In Dean's case, it was success and promotion. I could see why Dean said we needed a lot of new blood in the organization, and Andy's suggestion made sense. Maybe we could spark things up to bring in the talent.

Still, it was early in the game for both Andy and me to shake up the whole scene. So I answered him but did not answer him, if you know what I mean. "It's a good idea, but I don't feel too qualified yet."

"What's this about changes?" asked a lanky blonde chick who had been standing near us. We were by the pool, and she had been talking to a very distinguished gray-haired man. Evidently she had been listening to our conversation, too, and I was glad I had not said too much.

"Oh, uh, Mike, this is Charlotte," Andy said. "She used to be a brother, but well, they had something more important for her to do."

Brother! Some brother. Lanky or not, she had a regal bearing. There was a quality about her I could not quite analyze. She was smartly dressed in a black net, low-cut cocktail gown, and she seemed to exude some kind of special power. Maybe it was her eyes. Even in the dim lights of the tiki torches around the pool, they radiated a purple light of their own.

"If there are any changes to be made," she said, smiling sweetly, "it would be a good idea to get my suggestions before instituting them. I might be able to see flaws that you overlooked or advise you on how to sharpen them up."

"Yeah, well, I was just telling Andy that I wanted to see how things worked out first." I was nervous while talking to her. It was those eyes.

"You're a smart boy, Mike. You'll catch on fast."

71

"Sure."

She turned away, and I thought, "Not you, baby; I like tigers, but I'm not sure I'm ready for a devil cat."

When she was out of earshot, Andy whispered, "That's one from the fourth step, and you'd better watch your step around her. She's power, man!"

"The fourth step?"

"Yeah. Some people think it's the *Illuminati*, but you'd better not breathe that word to anyone!"

Someone was calling my name—"Mike! Mike! Oh, there you are. I've been looking all over for you. Have you had enough for one night?" Dean asked.

"Yeah, man. I'm really beat. I think I'll sleep good tonight. That is, if you don't have any errands for me." I had learned all I could from these people here. I wanted to remember their faces and the names they had given—whether they were the right names or not—something to call them by the next time I saw them. One of my good points was putting names and faces together, and it always impressed someone to think you had remembered their name. Without seeming too curious, I was able to find out that among those present were a few teachers, some locally prominent people, and a city official.

By the time Dean and I left for our apartments, I felt light-headed. The fact that the ceremony had gone so smoothly and I was the new Master Counselor gave me great satisfaction. I did not expect it to be easy, and I knew with this crowd, there would probably be more demands put on my time than before. But I felt it would be worth it. I was in a position of power.

Dean dropped me off, saying, "This car, with a driver, will be yours tomorrow. I've noticed your driving has become erratic lately, possibly because of the heavier work load and the amount of speed you're taking, and we don't want anything to happen to you."

"Yeah, that's a big help," I answered. "Just the other night, I had a narrow escape coming back on the Riverside Freeway. Almost fell asleep at the wheel and tooled off onto the shoulder before I realized it."

After we reached my apartment, Dean leaned over and gave me the handshake of the Brotherhood. "Good luck, old buddy, and good-bye. I'm headed 'Frisco way on the first plane out, so I won't be around to pester you anymore."

His farewell and manner of giving it surprised me, but I did not show it. You were not supposed to show feelings. "Say, those top dogs move fast, don't they?" I commented. "Where do I get my supplies now?"

Dean laughed. "You'll see; everything will be supplied now," he answered mysteriously.

"Good deal. Take it easy."

As I walked upstairs, I noticed a light showing through my window, and I had not remembered leaving the lights on. I opened the door cautiously, looked in, and thought I was in the wrong place. Where there had been flimsy curtains at the windows, now there were gorgeous drapes.

A long, low, oxblood leather couch replaced the sagging old brown horsehair one, and there were two sets of bookshelves full of books beneath the windowsill where there had been a rickety scarred table. The biggest surprise was on the floor—two chicks sitting on a white rug.

"Oh, wow," was all I could think of to say. "Did you two do all this since I left for the meeting?" I went over and sat on the soft couch, feeling the smoothness of the leather. "Who knew the type of furniture I like?" In my casual conversations, I probably had mentioned being attracted to certain types of furnishings, colors, etc. But I could not help thinking of Satan's power, and my experience with the wishing smoke which Teresa had concocted for me.

The girls just grinned and came over and sat on each side of me. "We hope you like it, Mike, because we come with the apartment," said the blonde one named Lorraine. My mind was racing ahead, trying to figure out if this was what Dean meant. Did they expect to stay here, too? I had only one bedroom, but Dean had mentioned I might get an "extra" apartment.

"Mike, you look tired," the other girl, Sandy, said.

"Would you like me to fix a little pick-me-up? A supply of groceries was put in the kitchen tonight."

"Man, I sure would," I said. "If I'm going to get through the rest of this night, I'll need plenty of chow."

While she was fixing my snack, I browsed through the books that had been furnished. I was pleased to note that many of them were on the occult and included several I had previously consulted at the library. Now I would not be hampered by having to run back and forth to the library.

The next week just flew by, with the girls helping me pick out a new wardrobe of clothes and a complete set of china and silverware. The biggest acquisition of our shopping trips was a stereo set which had everything, I mean, everything. The manager of the store evidently was on the fringes of the "movement" and said whatever I chose was mine. "Get what you want. Don't settle for second-best, Mike," he said. "If I don't have it here, I'll put it on order." He had what I wanted, and it was delivered that same day.

The apartment was pretty crowded. Part of one corner had to be turned into an office, and there were a lot of people coming and going on "coven business." The chicks did a good job of keeping the place neat and tidy.

The study of ritual fascinated me, and I ran across several things that I was not sure the other members would know, so I called a few brothers together and we went over them. "You're the ritual leader," Paul said. "We'll take your word for it, and whenever you want to try something new, just do it, and then if anybody objects, we'll bring it up at the regular meeting."

But I still held back. I was afraid to rock the boat too much right away. In most situations, Mike Warnke was a pushy guy. I always pushed my way to the front of a line. But not in Satanism. Not yet. To be honest, I was running scared. I remembered Teresa and the power she invoked, and Charlotte with those eyes, those purple eyes. But I did plan a few minor changes, changes that I hoped would make the ceremony more clear and to the point.

I appropriated some ideas from the Catholic church. Much of their ritual still impressed me, and now that I had a chance to pervert it, I was going to do it. Part of our code was to pervert hallowed Christian tradition deliberately and viciously.

I had been assigned a personal messenger, and I found that since I did not have to drive anymore, I had much more time to devote to learning witchcraft and the rituals that would be coming up in my first meeting in just a few days.

The other Master Counselor, who was to be replaced soon, was a great help, as he was in charge of all the business, like paying for my apartment, ordering supplies, keeping up with the sales, handling correspondence, and being in charge of the huge box containing all the robes, equipment, and supplies for rituals. He was the one who was responsible for getting the altar back and forth to our meetings. He seemed to be a steady and dependable kind of guy, but I did not press him about whether he was going down or up when the new brother stepped into his place. He was not a talker, anyway, any more than Andy was. I had a green light to be spokesman of the group— Mike and his mouth.

Well, I was determined that our group would be different, eventually, and if I had to spend twenty-four hours a day out crusading for the Brotherhood to get the right kind of members, I would. Dean had also warned me that the coven had to be kept active, busy, and happy, or there would be trouble. What kind of trouble, he did not say, but I could guess.

The day before the first meeting at which I would preside, I still felt touchy about how to call on those demonic spirits. I had already read one case where two jokers had been fooling around and had stood in the wrong part of the circle, with their toes on the pentagram, and the demons had crushed them to death. Their rib cages had caved in like balsa wood under an elephant's foot. Exactly the same thing had happened to both of them. They were twins in death.

I did not want my first meeting to end that way! I went around practicing the words I was supposed to use to get the demon back where it belongs. I also had to make sure the pentagram was freshly painted on the altar stone every week so there would be no break in the lines forming it. If there was a break, a demon could get out, becoming a wild and unfettered demon. That would be dangerous.

Meeting night came. I decided I had better have an extra shot to keep my nerves calm and appear the way Dean had. On second thought, I decided to program myself to project my own personality at its best. I concentrated on this as I popped some speed, hoping to give my subconscious mind a fix on it. Paul and Andy, my fellow counselors, had gone early, to set everything up right. The heavy stone altar was in place, the Great Mother and goat's head were on their stands with two candles burning beside the altar. The incense burners were filled and burning. It was good to be on the inside running the whole show, and it gave me a feeling of power. I glanced at the ring on my left index finger before the ritual started and hoped it would be a real focus for Satan.

The ceremony got under way without a hitch, and the other two Master Counselors knew exactly what they were to do and did it, taking that worry off my back, leaving me free to concentrate on raising a demon.

As I started the ritual for raising a demon, as I had seen Dean do so many times, the thought went through my mind that most people outside of witchcraft and Satan worship do not even believe in demons. So many people refuse to believe until they see or feel something for themselves. By the time our ceremony was over, any skeptic who could have viewed it would have been made a whole-hearted believer. I was proud of myself for pulling it off without a hitch.

As members of the Brotherhood, we probably understood demons better than most people, because we used them to accomplish our evil deeds. Demons are Satan's helpers, fallen angels who were expelled with him from heaven. They are an invisible presence. You cannot see them, but you soon know they are there. There are legions of demons. No one knows how many. Perhaps some demonologists could name all the *commanders* of legions of demons, but the rank-and-file outnumber people!

Some groups have favorite demons on whom they call again and again to afflict their enemies. They call, "Master So-and-So," or "Master Such-and-Such," and then ask for the favor they have in mind. The demons have to do what they are commanded, but like rebellious children, they resent their obligation to serve you. You have to know the proper way to safely unleash a demon, for they will stomp on you, to put it mildly, if you forget any of the safety measures.

In our ceremonies, we called on demons to do almost everything a person's Satanic-oriented mind could dream up. We had control of a Satanic power, although often demons themselves do their own destructive deeds without our help in directing them.

Demons can inflict disease, can possess men, can possess animals, can oppose spiritual growth, can disseminate false doctrine, can torment people, and can be tormented by people. Demons can talk or can cry with a loud voice, using the tongues and lips of humans. They can tell lies and make people believe lies. They can even preach. They can stand, walk, and seek rest when embodied in a human being. They can tell fortunes, make people strip off their clothes, cause suicides, render a person insane, or cause a body to be bowed in affliction. They can cause jealousy, pride, or lust. They can drive a person into despair.

Demons seek to inhabit human bodies that they might work out their indescribable lusts and evil longings. They will not willingly leave a human they inhabit. If cast out, they will seek to re-enter the same body, inviting other demons to join them. It is known that as many as two thousand demons inhabited one man.

After the meeting, several members of the coven came up to tell me how well I had performed for the first time. I was still nervous, and I was glad there had not been too many problems to discuss. We had to call on the demons only once, and that was enough.

"Say, Mike," Paul said, "will you give me a hand with this altar?"

"Sure, Paul. Be right there." I went over. "For the love of the devil, what did they make this slab out of, and where did you get it? It weighs a ton." We heaved the piece of black marble granite into the back of Paul's pickup, then the heavy box of robes and rituals items.

"We got this hunk of granite from a monument company," Paul explained. "It was a remnant. Some guy near Fontana just practically gave it to us. It was all polished up and cut to size, only it turned out to be the wrong size for the particular customer, and he did not know what to do with it."

"Man, that would make a good coffee table with its rough-hewn edges, and it's at least six inches thick. No one could knock that over." I shook my head. "I think I'll go and pay that guy a visit. A table like that would sure go well with my new couch."

By the time we had everything loaded, the place was empty, and it was an eerie feeling standing around that old barn with no one except Paul and me. I had decided earlier that this would not be the night for fun and games. I had one delivery left to make—a big one—and it could not be trusted to one of the new messengers, so I wanted to be well-rested for the occasion.

The next morning, my messenger picked me up, and we drove down almost to the border of Mexico. The Brotherhood was handling a large percentage of the drug traffic for the Inland Empire area of Southern California. So this pickup and delivery was badly needed. Dean had said there would not be any more errand-running, but when there was a lot of money involved, I would have to be along when a new guy was being broken in.

We got the stuff and delivered it to an address in Ontario, on the fringe of our area, to divert any suspicions, and got back into town just ahead of the heavy afternoon traffic. As soon as my driver, Hank, let me off and started for the parking lot, two cops jumped me. I was not sure just what to do in this case, having the $5,000 in my billfold. I should have stashed it in the car.

"If you get into our car without a lot of trouble," the redheaded cop said, "you might get this thing taken care of right away."

I was skeptical, but I knew they would get a search warrant and turn my apartment upside down if I demanded my rights, so I said, "Sure."

Once inside the squad car, I was confronted by the two cops. "We're concerned, Mike, with the fires you've been having without a permit," the older cop said, offering me a cigarette.

I almost fell through the floor. "Oh. Well, what's the procedure for getting a fire permit? A burning permit?"

The officer grinned. "Well, why don't you invite us down to one of your weinie roasts? Frankly, we'd like to get in on some of the action. Oh—" he waved his hands as I made an instinctive motion toward my pocket—"I don't mean any direct cut or anything like that. But if you'll let us offer you any help you might need to keep your thing going smoothly, you see, it will put *us* in contact for some profitable diversions. Any guy you people have trouble with might lead us into something interesting. I think we can work together harmoniously. Live and let live is our motto here."

We came to an agreement, and the red-haired cop opened the car door letting me out to walk back to my apartment. I could not help smiling. Money really swings it, I thought. I would worship Satan harder than ever. I wondered just how many other people they let off with a little payola or cooperation. This is something every town fears and many citizens worry about, but in the places where you run across it, the actual example is hard to believe. It proves how strong Satan is, getting his horns in there where it really counts.

I still was not sure just what angle the local fuzz planned on playing, but I was going to be more careful, though knowing the police were on our side was going to make a difference. I will be able to put the Brotherhood on the map for sure, now, I thought, and make our organization top-dog.

My two girls were waiting for me with a hot meal and the message that a guy had stopped by to inquire if he could see me tomorrow. After they had finished describing him, I guessed it was an old school buddy of mine from Crestline.

The girls assured me that they were careful not to divulge any information about what I was doing, though they were basically in the dark themselves, but Sandy said my visitor had been quite interested in my occult library. Lorraine had told him that, since I seemed to have a lot of people coming and going, she was sure it would be all right if he came back the first thing in the morning.

Since the girls were just there for show and for my pleasure, I never discussed my plans with them. But I said, "Look, girls, from now on don't let anyone in that you don't know if I'm not here. I don't want anyone snooping around my things. You can play your little hostess games with my friends like the higher-ups told you to, but with a stranger, just play it cool and pretend that you don't know anything. That shouldn't be too hard."

I still was not sure how much to tell these gals, or how to treat them. I knew they were just considered menials, or slaves, or whatever, and I was not sure how bright they were or how much they could be trusted.

We had just had our breakfast the next morning when my old buddy arrived. I was as surprised as he when I opened the door. "Carl! How in hades did you find me here?" I exclaimed, ushering him in.

He was a buddy from my drinking days back at high school, one of the ones who had answered some of the questions I had about other churches. He was taken aback for a minute with the different appearance I presented. I had not seen anyone from high school days for quite a while, and my long hair and the faint line of the mustache I was babying along really made me look different.

"I was just in town for a few days," he said. "And I

wondered if you wanted to go back up to the old 'home-stead' area around the lakes and goof off a bit. I've just accepted a good job back East, and I leave tomorrow. I didn't think it would be too much fun going up in the mountains by myself. My parents divorced and moved away in two different directions last year. So there is no one close up there."

"Sure. I'll get ready." I figured I had earned a day off, and it would be kind of interesting to see the old place with him. "Do you have any wheels, or shall I get my driver to take us?"

"Oh, I've got the old buggy out there. I've sold it, but the guy was nice enough to let me use it until I leave." Carl gulped. "Did I hear you say, 'driver'?"

"Uh, yeah. I'll explain on the way." I went into the kitchen and had Sandy give me a shot. I did not want to run out of steam halfway up the mountain.

We drove in companionable silence before Carl finally said, "Listen, ole buddy, what kind of racket are you in, anyway? That nice apartment, two girls at your beck and call, a driver, nice clothes, and furniture. I couldn't help noticing those books yesterday. Anything to do with that?"

"Well, I guess since you know half the story, I could tell you more, but if I ever find out that this got around——"

"Hey, now, Mike. You can trust me. Besides, I'm heading East, remember? Don't know anybody here any more and could care even less."

Carl took the curves with ease as we headed up the road to Crestline. The sky had been gray, but as soon as we reached the crest of the mountain, both of us were amazed that everything was clear and the sky was actually blue. "I hope we don't choke to death on this clean air. Say, how about stopping at the Pine Inn for a nice cold beer? I could use one. Then you could tell me about this 'business' you're in." He frowned. "Oh, you're not twenty-one yet, are you?"

"That's all right. I have a card that says I am."

He pulled into the parking lot, and I was surprised

when I opened the door to get out. I had just thrown in a lightweight jacket, and I put it on quickly as the air was nippy. It was not time for snow, yet, but it made me realize how close we were to Christmas, and how fast the time had been passing since I had begun working about twenty hours a day.

"Are you sure you and I shouldn't have a hot toddy?" I asked. "You forget how warm it stays down in the valley compared to the mountains. I wonder if they'll get snow up here by Christmas." I winced. The word actually sounded foreign on my tongue.

After we got inside and ordered a hot drink, I began to unravel a bit of the mystery Carl was waiting to hear. I told him just enough to impress him, but not enough to give anything away or to put the finger on the group or implicate me in anything.

Getting back into the car, heading for another one of our old haunts, Carl said, "I find all of this hard to believe." He laughed. "If you're really in witchcraft, put a hex on that building over there so it'll burn."

I thought he was kidding at first, but he said this with such a straight face, it rankled me, and not to be doubted, I said, "Pull over here and I'll show you." There was a small bar across the street. I called up a spirit and ordered it, "Burn down that building across the street. So mote it be." Then Carl and I got back into the car and drove off.

It was hard to tell whether he believed me or not, so I did not say any more as we left the scene. We drove all around Lake Gregory and spotted a number of places where we used to hang out. There were many new developments around the lake area, so it was hard to recapture that old feeling I was looking for, especially speeding through so quickly. "I guess it's hard to go back, Carl. Nothing is ever the same. Do you mind if we head back for the valley? I really should be getting back to work and be on call in case someone needs me."

"Sure. Anything you say. I thought there would be more to do up here, but I guess some of those places we used to drink and dance in are closed down now."

"Drink and dance! Hah! Those were the coke and cut-up days. You and I always managed to spike those cokes, though, didn't we, with the old bottle-in-the-inner-coat-pocket trick."

"Looks like you're still up to your old tricks," Carl commented.

As we headed back toward Crestline, we were passed by the emergency fire truck and a Forest Service van. They were in a big rush and honked for us to pull over. "They act like they're going to a fire," I commented. "I wonder whose?"

"Let's follow and find out," Carl suggested. Before he had my consent, he was already tailing them. They were just pulling in as we rounded a curve, and we could see that it was the bar I had hexed. Smoke was pouring out of one end, and people were running around trying to put out some open flames already starting at the roof line. Right in front of the bar, the fire truck had just pulled up, and two men got out and began unrolling a large hose. No one was going too close, because there were two butane tanks there. Suddenly, flames belched out of two of the windows, and part of the roof crashed in.

"Oh, my *God!*" Carl gasped. "I—I didn't really believe you, Mike."

"Don't go too close, Carl. Some of those people might recognize me, and I haven't been around here for some time. Haven't even seen my folks lately. In fact, maybe you had better back off and go around the other way." I felt shaky inside, shaky at my own power and at the thought that I had caused that scene.

Carl backed up, turned around, and went back through a shortcut we knew about. "Man, you'd better be careful with that stuff." Carl's voice was awed. "Someone might have gotten hurt." He did not say anything else for a long time.

I was nervous and jumpy by the time we got back—way overdue for another fix. Carl had not noticed the change too much, and by now, I was glad I had not said anything about the drugs. He was a pretty straight guy, after all. I had had it in the back of my mind that he might be a good contact for us after he got settled in the East, but after the fire, he seemed anxious to get back to the valley and drop me off. Maybe it had really scared him. He did not even give me his address in the East.

That was the last time I bothered with anyone outside the witchcraft group unless I felt they were definitely going to be a potential brother. We had discovered Christians were a complete waste of time, and we had already learned to leave them alone. Even the demons could not get to them if they had enough faith to ward them off. However, many Christians do not exercise their faith over demons; in fact, they do not even believe in them.

Although Satanists believe there is a God—to believe in Satan you have to believe in God—they have become alienated from believing that God's representation of "good" is the only way to fly. They believe God is good, but they don't believe that "good" itself is good. They do not want to wait until they die to get the rewards that heaven offers—maybe, if they are really pious and all goes well. No, they are impatient and, impetuously, want a little bit of heaven right here and now, while they are alive to enjoy it—heaven in the form of kicks, chicks, and checks, along with the agonizing ecstasy of drugs.

By the time our next meeting came around, I was much more familiar with the setup, knew more people who might be interested in joining, and, in general, had a lot to show for being in the organization only a short time.

This meeting was held inside, as it was getting colder. I had a call from Charlotte that someone would be coming to give us a message about some business that should be taken care of. She was quite mysterious when I asked her who it would be. I learned that where Charlotte was concerned, when she wanted you to know something, she would tell you. "Okay, baby, I'll play it your way," I thought. "Maybe someday we'll see who ends up on top."

Everyone was standing around talking. Then I gave the

signal to robe up, and the men went to one side and the women to the other. The barn was drafty when we started to undress, and there was much joking about getting warmed up afterward.

When everyone was in his place, I started the meeting with the ritual of the pentagram, voicing the chant, incensing the knives and other things that we used. Then the incense was reinforced with some new stuff. The girl lay on the altar, ready for the sacrifice. I pretended to disembowel her.

When it was time for the petitions to be brought up, a well-dressed gray-haired man stepped forth and said, "We have a problem. A certain professor at Valley College is going around the campus saying witchcraft is a bunch of baloney, and that we are crazy and liars. I would strongly suggest that you take appropriate measures to correct this gentleman. His name is Professor Dunn. But instead of going through him . . . well, he has two daughters in grade school. It might be effective to let him know of our presence through them." He sat down, and I felt uneasy as I stared at him.

Where had he come from? Who was he? I looked over at Andy but got no help. Paul nodded for me to go on, that it was all right, and then I remembered Charlotte's message.

"So this is how we get some of our orders," I thought. I let the meeting be open for discussion, and when everyone agreed that this professor had to be taught a lesson, I called for a vote. All ring hands were raised. No one placed his hand on the floor signifying a *no* vote. And all their eyes were on the stranger.

I went over and stood before the Great Mother with outstretched arms and began the chant. The group responded, their eyes on me again. I continued with another chant. "Master, we petition you, in the name of our Lord Satan, to afflict Professor Dunn's daughters so that he may know of our power." This was repeated three times. I waited. The room was very quiet. Then I felt the demonic presence leave the pentagram. The waiting had made me tense, and I was relieved when the presence left.

The sacrifice had gone well, and everything else about the meeting was just as I had planned. When it was over, I looked around for the gray-haired man but he was gone. I was glad he had not hung around, but did wonder who he was. I guess he figured he did not have any time to waste.

It was hard to get with it. After the meeting, I had my pick of girls that night, but I kept thinking about that "other group." How many times would they bug me? What would they ask for next?

I felt deflated, actually. With just the brothers of the coven around, I was big. Really big. But a guy like that gray-haired joker distracted my people from *me*. I felt like I was shrinking, like something out of *Alice in Wonderland*.

Maybe if I took some direct action on my own, I would get that feeling of authority back. I was determined to stay on top of it. I phoned several of the brothers. "Bring a butane torch. I think George has one. We're going out to the prof's house and burn an inverted cross on his front lawn just to make sure he knows who's afflicting his kids." After repeating it several times to different guys, I was hoarse. We would get in some licks of our own, right along with the devil.

That still did not make me feel any better. I was still hoarse. I was a mess. I told my chicks, "Why don't you two split for a few days. I want to be alone for a while."

They thought they had done something that displeased me and begged me to tell them what it was and how they could make it up to me.

"Just go," I growled.

Chapter Six

Listening to Andy's description of the professor's conversation, late in the afternoon, I could picture the prof's kids as they squirmed and cried while the red welts appeared on their arms due to demonic attacks, right under the professor's eyes.

Later, thinking about the scene between the father and his children made me think of my step-parents again. It had been months since I had seen them. The day Carl and I had driven up there, I kind of had it in the back of my mind to stop in, but after starting the fire, I did not want to be seen around there! It seemed easy enough to strike a pose when I was trying to recruit some naïve joker. But, the nostalgic associations which several hours with my parents could evoke might put me under a nervous strain that could easily result in my blurting out too much.

It was as if I had two distinct personalities: one kept telling me, "Stay away, man. You'll just hurt them some more."

The other personality, if let loose in their presence, would delight in doing that very thing—hurting them by vainglorious braggadocio in vile words and gestures. I learned later that this was demons' work. Unknown to me, the demons I had worked with had entered me and increasingly seized chances to get back at me for the labors I put them to.

Nevertheless, the craving to return to my parents again

was there as an undercurrent. One day a girl I had known since high school, Chris, whom I had invited to a straight party or two, said, "You know, I still live in that house in Cedar Glen across the street from the cocktail lounge—my old man still works there. That shed and garage on the bottom floor would be a perfect place to have a party or something. The owners wouldn't mind."

Cedar Glen was close to home! I could get that feeling of re-visiting my old haunts again, satisfy part of my longing to be near my step-parents and still not really give in to such blasé sentiments as homesickness. It would be a nice diversion.

"But how about the people who live in the other part of the house? Aren't you still sharing that house with a couple of other families?"

Chris shrugged. "No sweat. Part of the house is vacant right now, and the Hudsons are drunk all the time. If you shut the doors on the shed and garage, no one would know what was going on."

I hoped not. Chris had only a vague knowledge of my involvements. I do not know if she was even hip to the sex bit that was so much a part of the lives of my companions and myself. But I was not thinking in terms of a party which would be an orgy. That would be asking for it. The location, however, would make a perfect place for a coven meeting. We conducted our meetings quietly, and there would be no goofing around. Afterward, we could go to the Back Room to dance and just be sociable.

As a leader, I was entitled to all the recognition and luxuries I wanted from my people. On the other hand, keeping them motivated, interested, enthusiastic, and entertained was my responsibility and a hard one at that. Having a meeting up in the mountains would kill two birds with one stone!

Despite my desire to return to the setting where I grew up and the satisfaction of hitting upon a popular diversion for my group, I was tense as I approached the two-story red house set in among pine trees on the north shore of Lake Arrowhead. I was sitting low in the back seat of the

Continental, not anxious for acquaintances from the past to see me. I grumbled to my driver, Hank, to slow down. "It's right across the street from that restaurant," I said, pointing a finger. "There it is!"

Some of the others had already arrived, and I winced, seeing they had to park in plain sight, except for the first two or three cars, which had been able to drive down a gravel road and be more obscure.

I did not do a very good job conducting the meeting that night. It was a brief meeting but, even so, I was nervous. Having it so close to my old home was not a good idea at all; in fact, it made me feel lousy.

After the meeting, when we got together in the Back Room, my depression deepened. As we danced, I saw several of the local yokels I had known while living with my parents. I felt uncomfortable among them. Sure, I probably had more money and freedom than any two of them —a far cry from the days when my coke-drinking was limited by my meager earnings.

Later on, at home, when I took a downer so I could sleep it all off and maybe have some compensating pleasant dreams, I said aloud, "What Mike Warnke needs is to keep movin', man! When I'm really up there, even those guys and chicks on the mountains will have to look *up*."

I had been a Master Counselor for only a short time, and already I was dissatisfied. Yet I knew I had much to do to overcome the competition to get up higher still. That vague, mysterious, fourth stage was a ghostly thing, something few even whispered about. How could I get up there when I did not even know what it was all about?

I had to make *my* group the best: streamline the workings of my organization and then show it off before others, arouse their envy—and evoke the approval of that super-organization of which I suspected we were more a part than anyone realized.

In my dreams, Charlotte Smith appeared, a golden-haired goddess in a lacy black dress, with a hazel-branch wand and those scary violet eyes that had blazed out at me —"Remember, Mike, if you'd like any suggestions . . ."

She was up there—wherever *there* was. And she seemed to approve of me. Maybe I should take up her offer. It was a strange sleep, confused with traces of the high that still lingered, the soothing effects of the "red" I had taken, and the deep depression I had experienced.

In the clear light of the next day, however, I was not quite sure I should risk telling Charlotte what I had in mind and ask for her help. You were not even supposed to acknowledge that a person was in a particular position in an organization which, as far as the world was concerned, did not even exist. You were supposed to wait to be called.

I had a busy day, studying some occult books in the morning under my tree at the college and also considering a list of names of possible recruits and noting what I knew about them and what progress I had made in delving into their backgrounds.

In the afternoon, at the job I retained as a cover, I dealt out hamburgers until I wished I had never seen one, my mind drifting into dark corners far from the smelly greasy little stand on the corner of a noisy street. In the evening, I enjoyed a steak dinner at a classy restaurant in Riverside, talking with one of my "prospects," whom I was treating in preparation to springing the Melanie routine on him. When I got back from that and several drinks at a local bar, I breezed up the stairway to my apartment and unlocked my door. Even before I switched on the lights, I sensed someone was in that room ahead of me. It was Dean! He was sitting at my desk, his feet propped up, with my notebook open in his hands. He shut it with a snap and plopped it down when the lights went on.

"I didn't expect you so early," he said, glancing at the clock. It was only ten-thirty. "I was—thinking—so hard that I didn't hear you unlock the door."

"I didn't expect to see you around again," I said. "I thought you'd be in Mississippi by now."

"I am. That is, I'm en route. The training session is over. I'm between planes." He slid his feet off the desk and dropped them noiselessly to the floor. "I was just waiting for you to tell you I think you're right-on. Just keep up the 'bad' work and don't telegraph your punches. If you have a hunch, act on it. Well, I've got to get going." He gave me the Brotherhood signal—the one with the little and index finger extended—instead of accepting my offered handshake.

"Wait a moment," I said, turning to get the note pad I kept by the telephone. "How about giving me your address in Mississippi?" But when I turned around, he was gone. It was an incredible performance of speed, getting from around my desk in the far corner of the living room and out the door in such a short time and without a sound. I hurried to the hallway and then to the head of the steps, but he was already out of sight.

Dean's conversation encouraged me. From here on in, I would pull out all the stops.

The next day, as I leaned against the eucalyptus tree on the campus of San Bernardino Valley College, I saw Charlotte swinging past. "Hey, Char," I called, clambering to my feet with the aid of the tree trunk. "Hold it, will you?" I hurried over to her and walked with her toward the steps of the Life Science building. "I just wondered if you have the time to talk with me about some ideas I have? The sooner the better."

"Sure, Mike. If you haven't got anything on tonight, I could drop by your place and we could talk."

"It's a date, then."

"See you later." She swept beautifully up the steps, and I went back to my tree. A guy was there waiting for me. He was one of my prospects. "I wasn't sure if you were holding office hours," he said. "Now, about that speech you were going to help me with—that lecture I'm going to make at the library on existentialism."

"Oh, yeah," I said, searching my mind for a moment. "We were talking about it Tuesday and got interrupted. Well, as I was going to say, I know this girl . . ."

For the rest of the day, I could not think about anything else but Charlotte. When she finally arrived, she looked exactly as I expected, only more so. I looked forward to the day when whatever it was she had would no longer intimidate me. As she accepted a highball and sat on my ox-blood couch while I draped myself over the chair, she said, "Every day, in every way, you're getting bolder and bolder."

I shrugged. "Like, I got to, to hold down my job."

"Sounds more like you want to hold it up, Mike," she replied. "Which is good. I think you could very well get rid of some of that archaic stuff, put a more mod appeal into the rituals. Use some acid-rock music to set the mood. Then you can shut off the music before you start the actual ceremony. Get a little handclapping into the meetings and, sure, go heavier into the blood and the bread.

"We've got some people who still go to Catholic Mass, then come down to the second stage," she continued. "They go to Mass for the status and because it's a front for the benefit of their parents, and so on, but they're hip with us and eager to do little jobs, like stealing communion bread laid out by the priests—"

"I was afraid you would think I was just trying to put the make on you, Char, suggesting we get together . . ." I laughed nervously.

For a split second, her eyes narrowed. She wet her lips with her tongue and continued, "And holy water. You know the procedure with the holy bread. After the Catholic priest has consecrated it to Jesus, the guy pockets as much as he can without the loss being noticed. Then we step on it to desecrate it and pass it around while we're drinking the blood, or whatever." Her nostrils quivered. "That's the scene. Write it in your book, Mike. I'm sure we'll—they'll—approve anything you come up with to promote this thing.

"After you've given it a fair shake, let me know, and we'll arrange for you to go around to some of the other groups and tell them about it," she indicated.

When she was standing at the door to my apartment, ready to leave, I put my hand on the knob to be holding onto something. She had a strange power, and just talking with her got to me. I was trembling all over. After saying "Good-bye," she didn't turn to leave, but hesitated, staring at me. She stepped closer, and I tensed. I did not know what to expect. She kept gazing at my face, my eyes, a slight frown creasing her forehead. "Mike—I happened to look closely at your eyes. When I look into them deeply . . ." She trailed off for a moment, and my throat went dry. "When I look into them, I see—a star and a crescent." She spun around and left. It was several moments before I realized I was still holding onto the doorknob. I closed the door and let go of it.

I was all set to spend the next few days preparing for a really swinging meeting during which I was going to propose all kinds of interesting innovations. Tonight would be for sleep, and the next day and the day after would be spent in intensive studies, frenzied note-taking, outlining little speeches I was going to make, deciding on whom I would delegate, for instance, to snatch holy bread from a church for use in our rituals.

Tonight I had been inspired, and I thought a good night's sleep would be just the thing to give me a fresh start. But, as so often happens on occasions like that, all my plans were messed up. Lorraine and Sandy came trotting back to my pad with their suitcases and told me how much they had missed me during their "holiday." They were right there in the flesh, reminding me—as if I needed reminding—of all the advantages of so-called belonging.

The next meeting was an outstanding success, and no one questioned the changes I made in the rituals. The Sunday preceding the meeting, one of our brothers, who was also fronting as a Catholic, got ahold of some holy bread and a fruit jar full of holy water. On meeting night, the other two Master Counselors and I made a good show of stepping barefoot onto the holy bread. We had already desecrated the holy water by sprinkling some urine in it.

The next step was to get some genuine human blood for our Communion. "Volunteers!" I barked. "Up to the altar." I picked up the ritual knife while Paul held a chalice ready to receive the blood. "I'll be first," I said, extending my wrist to allow Andy to make an inch-long slit. After letting the blood from my wrist trickle into the chalice, I turned to acknowledge the first volunteer, as Andy tied a strip of gauze around my wrist. "Come forward," I said, dropping my arm and stepping back.

After my example, other volunteers contributed to our blood bank, and we soon had a chalice half full. Then we added wine and the desecrated holy water. We three priests each took a sip, passing it from one to the other after first nibbling a piece of the holy bread, then passing the chalice to one of the guys in the circle to be handed around until each had eaten bread and drunk of the "wine."

A couple of the chicks seemed a trifle white in the face, and imagining their inner feelings at the taste of human blood gave me a sadistic pleasure. I was on the right track.

The higher-ups heard of our "improvements," and word filtered down to me that they were very enthusiastic. Charlotte came to one of our parties and stayed long enough to advise me that a bunch of people in the Victorville area would like me to come and tell them about our experiences. "Why don't you get a few of your second-stagers to go up there, too?" she suggested. "They're into the 'Earth Mother' stuff up there and not really hip on rituals and hard-rock Satanism. You could be a missionary to them."

"Great! When?"

"They're going to have a rock concert or something a few days from now, and as soon as I find out the exact day, I'll send a messenger . . ." She drifted away and I felt honored—and shaky. She still shook me.

A night or two later, about midnight, I was sitting on the couch with a fat book on formulas and incantations when—*flash!*—this chick materialized in the middle of my living room. I knew my door was bolted! My book turned somersaults to the floor, and I sat there frozen as solid as ice, my jaw almost touching the floor. I *felt* like a block of ice.

"I have a message for you. Char says it's on for Saturday afternoon."

I did not recognize the chick, except that I knew she was for real. I was not high; I was not hallucinating or flashing back. I fervently wished I was.

I had read about astral travel and Eckankar and knew that they were part of the occult bag, but I had written it off as 99 percent wishful thinking and one percent supernatural phenomena. Now the living proof was standing in the middle of my living room. What in hell had I gotten into?

"Well?" the chick said.

"Yeah, yeah. Okay. I got the message," I replied.

She seemed satisfied. Then, zap!—she was gone, just like that. The chills returned to my scalp and trickled down my spine. I got up and poured myself half a glass of Scotch. As I started to gulp some down, I tasted blood mixed with it, and the glass fell to the floor. I ran to the bathroom, my hand over my mouth. A glance in the mirror revealed my nose was bleeding. An involuntary moan escaped me that frightened me as much as anything that had gone before.

I had planned on using acid rock to keep our young crowd tuned in. Now we had a chance to renew our acquaintance of what was "in" with the hard-core hippie cult when we made the scene in Victorville.

Paul and I, along with two others from our group, decided to go up ahead of time, to jaw with the population. It was a welcomed trip. From the cold, drizzly, San Bernardino Valley, we wound up into the icy heights of the mountains and followed the wide freeway down into the dry hot air of the desert. It was at least ten degrees warmer as we passed the rocky northeastern base of the mountain range.

Thousands of acres of arid pink orange flatlands were interrupted by strips of lusher irrigated croplands.

As we neared our destination, we were passed more and more frequently by strings of motorcyclists. On the backs of their jackets were symbols indicating at least an appreciation of Satan, if not a worship of him.

Paul knew where we were headed and had Hank turn off on an ungraded road that went along a riverbed which had only a thin stream of water in it. Where level land fanned out in a broad valley dotted with scanty shrub, we found them, the flower children, blank eyes peering out through veils of hair.

They were camped there, conveniently near a dump from which could be procured scraps of lumber and cardboard to erect flimsy shelters. Some had moved wrecked, engineless cars to the riverbank to use as dormitories. Some were moving aimlessly down the road, tripped out. Others were awake enough to beat noise out of tinny guitars, and a few were animate enough to sway to the discordant rhythms.

We had to buzz around to a lot of flowers to discover the honey that was spokeswoman for this loosely organized group. When we found her, she was in a group listening to a guy strumming, "Black Is the Color of My True Love's Hair." She gave us her close attention when we told her we were from the Brotherhood. The guitar player missed a couple of beats, though he did not say anything, or register any kind of expression. I have never seen such dead eyes. Somehow, though, I sensed he was interested when we described our concept of witchcraft.

Taking us to one side, the chick said, "Junk like that bugs Sonny. He's so gentle. It's me that digs this Satanist bit. They——" she gestured vaguely toward the sprawling campers——"well, they worship the water, the earth, the sun, and the stars. But they ought to know who controls all of it.

"Myself, I think Lucifer is beautiful. Like . . . Sonny. They are free. But they don't know what they're free *from*. They don't know how to focus flower power. They think they're tuned in, but they're not really. Don't know how to get rid of their hassles. They say they're doing their own thing, but they don't know what their thing is. That's the point: their thing is——nothing. No thing! They're empty vessels." She looked out at the floating, drifting troupe, then turned back with new intensity. "And they're ready to be filled. You can fill them, Mike . . . Paul. Tell it like it is. Tell them about incantations and rituals. Maybe—" she laughed—"maybe even Sonny will dig it."

When it neared time for the blast, some pros in rock entertainment showed up. I waited to see what was going to happen.

Lydia, I think their leader's name was, had wrapped herself in a slinky silver sari and coiled some long beads around her neck by the time the rock group started to play. Making just a few circuits around the immediate area, I sold all the grass I had brought with me and then settled down to wait until Lydia stepped up to speak. She told the group about the "guests," and I got to my feet and made my way through the small crowd to where Lydia was standing.

Without mentioning names, I told them about "groups that I knew of" and what they were doing to get some real focus on power. Taking my cue from the words Lydia had used in describing to me earlier the "needs" of these people, I deftly manipulated the word *love* and described in glowing terms how beautiful Satan was and how faithfully he looked after his worshipers.

"You do for him," I pointed out, "and he does for you. When you get on a bummer, he's there to ease you. Have hassles? No sweat. He takes care of your cares. He gives you easy coasting and gives you a nice soft crash pad when you need it. Heard of the magic dragon? That's Lucifer, man! Ever hear of Pan? He's love, man. Free and easy love. Satan's cloven hoofs are from Pan, and Pan was the god of natural love and fertility. Satan's the pusher of all your heart's desires and pushes up the flowers of the earth. Well, all I can say, man, is: get with it. You know."

Naturally, I was interested in the feedback. I had no idea how I came over with that bunch, but as I analyzed it later, I guess it was a-okay. The flower kids picked up on certain words and did not really try to structure anything logical out of it. Mostly they were tuning in on my general expression of sympathy with their cause, whatever it was, and my appearing to share something *good* with them.

Lydia came to me after the "music" started again and said, "Mike, you really turned them on!"

I looked around. It was difficult for me to see this, but I guess she could read them better than I. Certainly I was willing to accept her word for it.

It was more important, however, that the fourth-stagers liked what I did there in Victorville, so when I got back, I tensely awaited some indication of their reaction. It was not long in coming. "You were right-on," was the consensus, and this time it was expressed by the tall guy with the spade-like hands whom I had almost run into the night when the trees tried to grab me. He met me outside the barn just before the next meeting and added, "You're a real traveling salesman for Satan, Mike, and we want you to go to Salem and get more hip with some really serious organization."

"What's at Salem besides a hanging tree?" I inquired, uneasy.

"A witch with a long family tree. An ancestor of hers by the same name was hanged there June 10, 1692, but don't sweat it, Mike, they don't do that anymore. Bridget Bishop has invited a bunch of high-level guys and chicks who'd like to get with it, and I recommended you. Call it a training session. All expenses paid, of course. Want to go?"

"Right on!"

Almost the next thing I knew, I was winging across the country in a jet. We landed in Boston, and I took a smaller plane to Salem. The meeting actually was not in Salem proper, but at Bridget Bishop's rambling, barnlike house somewhere out in the boondocks.

I was astounded at the number of cars parked around the house on the first day of the meetings, and at the different states represented on the license plates. Later, I learned there were about two hundred attending. Bridget Bishop was stunning, one of the most beautiful women I have ever seen—cultured, well-bred, an art enthusiast, a music-lover from the word go—as sweet a girl as you would ever meet . . . at one of these meetings!

But she was deadly serious about witchcraft, an authority on organization, with some ideas on the "step system" which she immediately began to expound.

It seemed a lot of us there at the conference had really been bringing in new recruits. I was credited with doubling the size of our group in San Bernardino from five hundred to one thousand in the short time I had been Master Counselor.

"But the fourth-stagers think you gentlemen aren't putting all that concentrated Satanpower to work," Bridget chided. "You're not doing enough with them, and you're not using proper security measures. If you don't improve your surveillance practices, one of these days, some novice is going to blow it for all of us."

Miss Bishop then proceeded to suggest ways of more systematically planting people from higher levels in the lower level—second- and first-stage functions. "You do a good job in getting these things started," she went on, "but do you stick around to see what's going on? You've got to know what's happening at all times. There's always someone in each level whom you could persuade to be an 'undercover' guy for the next lower level, to report back to your level the direction things are taking. There's always one in the crowd who enjoys the cloak-and-dagger bit. Make use of him or her. There are plenty of rewards to offer. We'll help out. Those above us will help out. That's another thing for all of you to consider—the rewards for making your particular group a model of modern witchcraft."

I sat there listening—and wanting to ask questions. It was not smart to ask questions. You always waited to be told. You just crossed your fingers and hoped your efforts would be rewarded. The main thing was that here I was, Mike Warnke, making the scene with the top people in witchcraft from all over the U.S. I was a big man among big men. I was there because my superior talents had been recognized.

I dug all the speeches and informal discussions. There was some talk of philosophy, of the might-makes-right variety. There was much consideration of successful organizational practices, much of it taken from business and military procedures. You almost forgot the diabolical nature of the movement around which the whole thing centered. It could have been a meeting of General Motors' board of directors. We could have called ourselves Satan and Sons, Inc.

My eyes were finally opened to the enormity and effectiveness of the Satan movement. I was now aware of the fact that I was part of a deep and widespread organization, operating not only in the U.S., but all over the world.

The word *Illuminati* was whispered around here, too, though it was still the wispiest of references. Was it indeed the fourth stage, the next higher level of Satan's superiors? Or—and suddenly an idea burst full-formed into my mind like a blast of light on a night sky—could there possibly be a *fifth* stage, that even fourth-stagers scarcely knew about and were forbidden to mention?

A worldwide, super-secret control group with perhaps as few as a dozen at the very top . . . with key men controlling governments, economies, armies, food supplies . . . pulling the strings on every major international event . . . and not just now, but for generations, centuries, since the beginning of civilization . . . manipulating men by their egos and their appetites, rewarding and depriving, enraging and pacifying, raising up first one side and then the other, maintaining a balance of frustration, bitterness, and despair . . . ?

Another rocket went off in my head. They did it through a Satanic knowledge of all the centers of self— self-love, indulgence, superiority, pride, righteousness— and they gently nudged the most ambitious and promising toward the final motivation-hook: *power* . . . for power was the *ultimate* lust, the thing that even an elitist would sell his soul for . . . and what better prize than power, the universal corrupter, for the more corrupt a man, the easier he is to control . . .

But the whole thing was too complex, too unpredictable . . . the most efficient human organization on earth could not possibly keep track of everything, let alone coordinate the amazingly intricate global causes and effects. And even more than that, the fantastically precise *timing* that would be required . . . *Blam!* I saw it. There *was* somebody who could mastermind the whole thing, and he had all the help he needed. Of course! *He* ran the whole operation! *He* worked out the details in the planning councils of hell, and sent his emissaries, like military couriers, on endless relays to the surface. Satan!

Even Christ Himself had acknowledged that Satan ruled the world. And in addition to the hundreds of millions of naturally selfish men who were doing his will by just being themselves, the one Christ referred to as the prince of this planet had a vast and growing secret organization of disciples who had pledged their souls to serving him—just to make sure things went as they were supposed to.

"Well, at least I'm on the right side," I thought. "And now Satan will *have* to promote me; I know too much."

Then one final, very unwelcome idea came into my head: if power was what motivated the most ambitious of us, and absolute power was what motivated the *Illuminati*, what motivated our unholy leader?

I was so badly shook that I was grateful for all the conference business to occupy oneself with, especially the big party planned for the conference conclusion. At the party, I planned to get to know some of the people from the East, South, and Great Lakes areas. Meanwhile, I took advantage of the free time during the remaining two days to explore a part of the United States that was unfamiliar to me and to talk with Bridget Bishop about art and classical music. She was as brilliant in these subjects as she was beautiful, except while talking about these subjects, she had a manner which like Charlotte's was charming on the outside, but left me with a vague uneasiness.

In her house were displayed art objects from both the U.S. and abroad. She had an antique chest which was so old, it was pure history—elaborately decorated in a style long since forgotten.

Then, too, she had a nail-studded door that her witch ancestor had erected. I did not ask her about that seventeenth-century Bridget Bishop, but in one of our discussions about art, when I mentioned a woodcut depicting a Salem Sabbat, she casually declared that some of the witch-hunters of Salem were actually witches, too.

Well, then, was her ancestor *not* a witch, but falsely accused and executed as one? Or had the former Bridget run afoul of her brother and sister witches and had her neck stretched for it? I felt a trembling in my shoulders. Or could it be that Bridget Bishop just lived on and on and on?

My conversations with her and close proximity to the scene where so much of witchcraft had made history prompted me to visit Salem. One old-timer pointed to a spot near a relatively new building. "That's where some of the witches were hanged," he drawled.

Another native gestured toward an old building that had been maintained in good condition over the years and said that one of the chief witch-hunters of former times had lived there.

My side excursion to Salem proper was too brief, and I did not have time to check these stories, but at least I felt I was on the spot where the witches and witch-hunters of old had done their thing. But having met Bridget, I was not sure which witch was which.

We had a swinging party at the end of the conference, and though the participants were close-mouthed about their specific activities, I had the feeling I was with people who knew where it was at—the good life—and how to get it. They were on top of a mountain!

Returning home, I had completely put out of my mind that night of hideous revelation and was filled with zeal and ready to tell my gang that we had to get with it by using our manpower more efficiently and effectively. I would tell them what rewards to expect for pushing everything from sex and dope to witchcraft and Satanism.

Just as I started to get down to the people, making personal visits and appointing "spies" to keep us informed of activities in the Brotherhood-at-large, I got notice of another impending conference at which my presence was desired!

I could not tell whether the impression I had made in Salem was so good that they wanted more of me, or whether I had flunked the test and they figured I needed further indoctrination. Anyway, it was a chance to travel some more and to see some more people. This one was to be in New York. They gave me a week to get ready. I decided to let things simmer on the home front while I took off for New York.

I landed at Kennedy Airport, rented a car, and zipped over to Queens. The man who had issued the invitations to the conference had a big house there. He was not an impressive character to look at, but he could well have been a leader, and he observed us as we elected a moderator and swung into our three-day conference. First, there was a planning session in which people proposed topics and the group as a whole, smaller than the one at Salem, decided when and how to schedule discussions on a particular topic.

Then we got down to earth. The purpose of the conference was a refinement of ritual, and all the planning boiled down to discussing incantations, formulas, gestures, occult effects, and performing various parts of the ritual. It reminded me of drama classes I had been in where someone would speak a few lines, then the others discuss delivery, context, and whatever. The idea was to get Satan's message across in a way that would appeal to young sophisticated malcontents.

I quickly saw how this New York conference was taking up where the Salem one left off. The one in Salem had concerned itself mostly with organization and security matters; this one went on to deal with the specifics of ceremonies and rituals. My innovations within my own group were brought to the attention of the conference, and they approved of getting more meaning into our services. One guy said, "Young people today are harder to get to. They've seen it all. You have to hit them over the head— shaft them with something that'll keep them involved."

Later, while having drinks in a local cocktail lounge, I got better acquainted with a guy I had talked to briefly in Salem. His name turned out to be Neville McCloud and he revealed a lot about himself—his favorite automobiles, how he liked his sex, the kind of women he made it with, his kind of clothes, what football teams he rooted for, and which hotels gave the best service. He really talked his head off about everything but witchcraft.

It was only right, though. I was careful not to drop any real facts about my dealings, my group, and my connections, either.

In the conference discussions, we never mentioned actual names, names of groups, exactly where the group was located, or anything like that. McCloud only indicated he was from "some place near the Canadian border." I was a "West Coast man," though most of them knew I was from Southern California.

The really big people, like Bridget Bishop, could afford to be a little more exact about some things. I guess they felt they had more leverage with really top people. The really big guys did not want to be bothered with trivial problems caused by small guys like me being indiscreet.

Small guy! I had these alternating feelings, first of being really top-dog as evidenced by my being selected to attend these conferences, then, by comparison to people like Miss Bishop, dwarfed. I particularly envied those shadowy people and people who kept especially quiet. Evidently some played the role of the public relations man or woman, allowing themselves to occasionally get in the public eye, and others worked very quietly behind the scenes with the more serious stuff. I envied them both. I determined to claw my way to the top. I intended to do this by making my home group so conspicuous to the shadowy guys that peeped in on us that no one could deny me the status and power I was after.

To keep up the mad pace, the flying back and forth across the country, the fourteen-hour-a-day sessions, the after-hours small-group meetings, the parties and the studying in between all this, I had started to do speed regularly in a big way. It kept me going, but it also did other things to me.

My two chicks said I was getting meaner all the time, and they seemed bent on escaping from their bondage to me. I did not even really know just how my benefactors kept girls tied down to being a guy's "slaves," and I did not ask, but I was getting tired of Lorraine's drivel. I asked Hank, my messenger, to convey to the proper people that I had seen another girl at a party that I would like to have as a replacement. Almost instantly, it was accomplished. Carmen was installed, and Lorraine sent out to the streets.

Several guys in Salem and New York had discussed the eating of flesh. I began to see that desecrating holy bread stolen from churches was kid's stuff. There were even some guys at the conference with missing fingers. They had sacrificed these to Satan.

We had initiated hypnotic rock music as a prelude to our rituals and encouraged heavier usage of drugs to get with it. We made sure fumes from our burners would add to the effect. Finally, I had developed a way to use my slick tongue along with a hypnotic tone to my voice, and I found I had my group eating out of my hand. It helped for them to know that I was a big shot with the higher-ups and frequently hustled off to lengthy conferences all over the map to meet with other practitioners.

At the next full moon, we went further than we had ever gone before. Part of me was in a state of almost unbroken revulsion, but the part that was in control was excited, to put it mildly. I knew there was nothing to do but relax and let the demons within me run the whole thing.

The flickering candles and flames from the surface of the crucible silhouetted me, as I turned slowly to the

Counselor of the Books and received from him a black leather bag that twitched and emitted muffled yowls.

At my nod, he reached into the bag and withdrew a cat, whose legs had been bound, but whose tail whipped about in a frenzy of terror. He held it up in the firelight to show the circle, and I raised the ancient sword that rested against the nude-adorned altar.

Around the circle, the others began to chant, their bodies swaying to the gradually accelerating rhythm. I intoned: "O Master of Darkness, accept, we plead, this our sacrifice of thanksgiving to thee, which we do dedicate to thee and to thy legion of demons, ad infinitum."

I swung the now screaming cat over the smoking caldron and then over the heart of the girl on the altar. Then, when the sword point touched the cat's belly, I thrust it in.

"Now!" I suddenly shouted, almost causing the wide-eyed onlookers to jump out of their skin, "I will draw the pentagram," and with my left index finger on which the large silver ring glowed, I drew an upside-down star on the girl's stomach, with the freshly spilled blood. From the weird utterances that now came from her mouth, I knew we were being graced by the presence of one of the denizens of hell.

Now I knew the time was ripe to ask them for some real evidence of their dedication to Satan. I had power, now, and I was going to use it. "You have contributed your own blood to the chalice, now we have a new request: we want your flesh," I told them. "Any of you guys not chicken, come forward, and let us see what you're willing to give to Satan."

We had a specially prepared board with nails in it to secure a guy's little finger away from his other fingers. To the side of the board lay a roofing axe. A guy came forward and slid his finger into the confining pattern of nails and closed his eyes.

I lifted the axe and brought it down with force. *Whomp!* His little finger, down to the second knuckle, remained on the board when he withdrew his hand. I left it to Andy to apply a simple tourniquet, and after giving him an opportunity to taste a bit of his own flesh, another guy drove the brother to the doc who was on our retainer-plus list.

Chapter Seven

It seemed that I had been home only a short while before I heard about a big meeting up in San Francisco. Though I had entrenched myself more strongly than ever with my own group through putting into practice some of my innovations, I still did not feel that I was getting enough indication of possibly being promoted into the fourth stage. Therefore, I asked to go to San Francisco, hoping I could learn more of the chain-of-command and make myself known in witchcraft in a big way. They said, sure, I could go, and they would pay my expenses.

The conference on the whole was disappointing. Unlike the previous secret meetings for Satanists, it was open to all types of occultists, and for me, it was like going back to kindergarten. There was one noteworthy moment at this conference, however; my encounter with Anton LaVey. He was pushing his Church of Satan which was only a "Rosemary's Baby" at the time. I was not impressed with LaVey; I detected a certain phoniness about him, but I admired his showmanship and decided I would show LaVey and his cronies that Mike Warnke could put on quite a show, too, and be one-up on the evil, even if my style was different from his.

I could hardly wait to get back to the group and tell them about the meeting and some of the new ideas I had picked up.

The flight home took only about an hour but, even so,

he time dragged. What if the plane should crash? The thought kept bugging me. There was one man on board with a red beard, and I suddenly thought of Castro. I signaled the stewardess, indicating I wanted to whisper something to her.

"I think there's a hijacker on this flight," I informed her. At first, she tried to explain that the new security measures had made this possibility very unlikely on this airline, but seeing I was persistent, she promised to speak to the pilot. I could tell I was making her nervous. It occurred to me that she would probably tell him I was paranoid, or something; it didn't occur to me that she was right.

We finally landed, and I took a smaller plane to the airport in the Valley and then phoned Hank that I was waiting to be picked up. I had a couple of smokes in the passenger lounge but finally went outside for the rest of the time because I felt people were staring at me. I felt very strange, not myself at all.

The girls had several messages for me when I got back. They were anxious to hear about the convention, but I was too tired to say much and hit the sack for some sleep. When I woke up, it was about eight o'clock, and suddenly I wanted some evening action. I called a few guys and chicks who belonged to the inner council and told them I wanted them to meet with me; like now, at the barn. "I want to try out a new ritual I picked up in San Francisco." We had a small candle-burning ceremony, and I tried a few formulas I had heard discussed, changing some of the words to see what would happen.

This one chick, Karen, suddenly started talking nonsense, interrupting what I was saying, just yakking about nothing. I had forgotten, but now I remembered that on a previous occasion, she had gone into possession. At that time, she had sat in one position for about five hours without eating, talking, or moving. She even urinated on herself. I watched now with interest to see what was going to happen.

It was not long before she went "ape." She started ripping her hair out in handfuls and tearing her clothes, rolling on the floor, and screaming. She was frothing at the mouth. She hit her head on something and broke a piece of tooth out while screaming and clawing at her face. I motioned for the others to restrain her, then bent down and started talking to her. I think I was merely transmitting something from Satan himself, because the words just suddenly came into my head without my thinking about them—

"You are one of my children, and I will take care of you," I said. "Don't worry about anything, because Papa is looking after you. We've got the power and riches of the world behind us, and we can't be conquered, so don't worry, because I won't let anything hurt you."

My words, my eyes, my tone, or something, seemed to soothe her, and she relaxed and slept awhile. We just left her there—she had her car outside—and later I found out she made it home all right.

At one of the secondary meetings I got to talk with my old friend the police officer, who was present with a young lady.

"Are you the guys who are killing all those dogs and draining their blood?" he asked me. "Reports on this have increased by 500 percent over the past three months." He shook his head. "Would you talk to your people? The whole thing is causing quite a litter problem."

I laughed. In my present state of mind, the cop's words were hilarious. I did remember suggesting to a couple of groups who were more or less grooming themselves to come into third stage that, if they could not get any volunteers for blood, there were always stray dogs around.

I remembered reading reports in the San Francisco paper about an increase in the number of dead animals found along the highways, so I guess it was not exactly confined to our area. In some cases, the incisions were made as expertly as any surgeon's—a "tribute" to our movement's students of this art.

In San Francisco someone had also suggested that when there was a scarcity of blood, menstrual blood could be used, but the priest had to urinate in it first. I mentioned this to the cop, but he did not laugh, for some reason.

At a regular meeting of the coven, the tall fellow with the big hands visited during the "business" session. "We have a problem we'd like you to take care of, ladies and gentlemen," the man said. "One of your members quit, and he's making a lot of noise. We're afraid he'll divulge some embarrassing things. We'd like you to take care of it on your level, if you can."

We all knew whom he was talking about. The guy had been deep in the drug scene, pushing, but suddenly developed cold feet or got fed up, conscience-stricken. We had been thinking about it, but no one had suggested taking any action. But when our mysterious stranger asked us to do something, we took it seriously. He stayed around long enough to see which way each one voted. It was unanimous. He left before we invoked a demon.

"Master," I said when the demon's presence was evident, "our former brother is straying. Convince him that silence is truly golden. Spare him no misery, Master. Make him see his duty to Satan, our father. Fire and pain shall be his portion. His bones shall be broken, and thus Satan will take pleasure. As I will, so mote it be!"

Later, we found out the demon had taken us at our word. In fact, the demon had really messed him up. I wondered if my own feelings, lately, did not somehow come across unconsciously and fire the demon's wrath more than we had intended, or if the demon was deliberately going beyond what it knew was our main purpose, to get back at me, or the group, for all the dirty work we had called on it to do. Or, perhaps, Satan was right now in the act of shafting me.

I had been told when I got back from San Francisco that our membership was now near the 1,500 mark and I could not imagine any reason why Satan would be displeased, except, of course, that night the pieces had come together. How I wish they hadn't! Remembering it, I had been getting a little nervous lately . . .

At any event, I was in a sober mood when the news was

splashed all over the papers, and it really gave me a jolt. It seems that the guy had been critically injured. His car had hit a bridge abutment and burst into flames. He had broken bones and burns all over his body. He had a bad concussion and would be in the hospital for a long time.

That night I woke up laughing. The vision of that crazy car swerving out of control, a demon grabbing the steering wheel from the driver and playing merry-go-round with it was too much! I had dreamt about the blood-splattered car and pavement and the big globs of blisters on the guy's body from the burns he suffered. Too much!

Sandy was leaning over me, shaking me awake. "It's 4:00 A.M. What's happening?"

"I just couldn't help thinking about the accident," I mumbled.

"At this hour? Weren't you asleep?"

"Oh, shut up and get me a fix."

She shrugged and started for the kitchen. Carmen still snored by my side, and I nudged her sharply in the ribs. "Get up and help your sister."

"She ain't my sister," Carmen yawned. But she got up.

While they were messing around in the kitchen where I stashed my layout and supplies, I suddenly sat bolt upright in bed. "Carmen! Sandy! What's *that?*" I shouted.

They came running into the bedroom. "Just the milkman downstairs."

"You're putting me on. *They're* after me."

"*They?*" they chorused.

"The Mafia. They're jealous because I control the grass."

"Mafia?" they chimed in again.

"Are you both parrots? Where's my fix?"

"We're still looking for it," Carmen answered. "Where did you put the speed?"

"Speed? I don't want speed. The *H*."

"H?" They looked at each other grimly. "You don't have any——"

"The hell I don't. I picked some up yesterday. It's stashed in the sugar can in the kitchen cabinet. Why don't you chicks use your damn heads?" I jumped out of bed and grabbed them by the hair and knocked their heads together. "You just need some sense knocked into you." I laughed. "Now, split."

They rushed off, crying, to the kitchen. I could hear them fumbling, pots and pans rattling. There was still that rattling coming from downstairs. I grabbed the phone and dialed Charlotte's number. "Char? Mike. You got to send over a couple of musclemen. Like, now."

"Mike? How'd you get my number?"

"I got it."

"What's the scene, Mike?"

"They're after me. The Mafia."

"You've got to be kidding. Hey, you know the time, Mike? It's four-fifteen. *In the morning*."

"You got to help me."

"They don't bother us; we don't bother them," Charlotte murmured.

The girls, pale and shaking, were standing in the doorway to my bedroom, watching me. They had the layout and the smack.

Charlotte said, "Didn't you hear me? I said, it's probably just the milkman. Go back to sleep or something."

"You see?" I groaned. "You're all against me." I slammed the phone down. "What the hell you waiting for? Fix me."

A couple of days later, I was sitting under my learning tree. It was a cool, gray day, and I was wearing a green topcoat, buttoned up to my neck. No one was outside. Suddenly, for no reason, I remembered the spring fog in the mountains. Tears came to my eyes. I buried my face in my hands and wept. "Mom," I cried.

Later, I looked up. Kids were hurrying to their next classes. Several were hovering around me. "You okay?" one asked timidly.

"Yeah. I'm the spy that's too dumb to come out of the cold." That was funny. I laughed. "Any of you guys want to buy some grass?"

They backed off.

"Oh? I'll give you some, then." I clawed up a hunk of turf and threw it at them as they turned and split. It was too much. I laughed.

At the next Brotherhood meeting, I could not wait to get to the finger chopping, but when it was time, it seemed suddenly horrible. They went on with it, though. I had really done a good job indoctrinating them. Chomp! Pass it around. When it was my turn to nibble at a tiny shred of that guy's finger, I gagged. They all looked at me.

Paul and I were talking the next day as we sat in his car at a drive-in hamburger stand. "Did you hear about that high priestess over in Gardena?" he asked, looking at me carefully. "She went berserk and was just about to blow their coven."

"What happened?" I asked.

"The higher-ups stepped in. Spread a little bread around in the right places. You know, the fixaroo. That hushed it up."

"What happened to the priestess?"

"I didn't ask."

"Well," I mused, "just shows what happens if you don't keep your cool."

"Mike, what are we going to do for that big sabbat next month? There are two new guys coming to be initiated into the coven. We ought to do something special."

My eyes had been following the swaying hips of a couple of cute carhops in miniskirts. "I know," I said, beaming. "I've been thinking for a long time— Every time I think about our *symbolic* sacrifices, instead of actually disemboweling the altar girl, I get up-tight. As Dean might say, 'We're short-changing the devil.'"

Paul shook his head. "No, man, that's too much."

I laughed. "I was only kidding. What I was really thinking—according to the *Book*, we're supposed to use an unwilling virgin. We're not doing it. Let's kidnap a broad and go through the fertility scene the right way. You know—lay her on the altar and take turns."

Paul thought a moment. "Now I'm with you. But we've

114

got to figure out how to keep her from shooting off her mouth."

"We'll give her a free home demonstration of demon power. She won't talk."

"Right on," Paul said.

An hour before the meeting, we were cruising along the streets in San Bernardino. Hank, the driver, and I were in the front seat, with Bert and James, our two strong-arm men, in the rear seat. On a side street, we spotted several chicks, some of them by themselves. They were all wearing raincoats, and we could see why—drops of rain started spotting the windshield.

"How can we tell if a chick is stacked, with all that rubber they're wrapped up in?" Bert complained.

"Search me," Hank responded, squinting through the windshield. On another side street, where it was darker, there was one lone chick on the whole block. "I think I know her," James whispered as we slowly passed her. "Go around the block, Hank, and we'll make a pickup."

I turned the car radio on, rather loud, to some rock music. Returning up the same block, Hank stopped the car just ahead of the girl as Bert and James jumped out quickly. "Hi, honey," Bert said, meeting her, blocking her path, while Hank, having gotten out on the street side, came up from behind. "How about a joyride?"

The chick knew someone was coming up from behind her. She looked quickly around the street. It was deserted. The shops and buildings were all dark. "Why not?" she said, as she decided not to resist. Her voice was shaky. In the car, she asked, "Where are we going?"

"We thought you'd like to be a guest at our meeting," Hank said.

The windshield wipers went *swish, swish,* and the music was going *bong, bong,* and I thought I could hear my own heart thumping from the excitement of what we had already done and were about to do. The girl's heart was probably pounding like the music, too.

At the barn, the girl zeroed in on the scene—she thought. "I was scared at first," she said as we strolled up to the circle. "But I know a little about you guys, and I know you're just a little weird like that. You know, swooping some girl up off the streets." She laughed.

I laughed, too. "I'm glad you're sympathetic to our cause. Get those clothes off now, and hop up on that slab."

"You've got to be *kidding!*"

"I'm dead serious. Hey, what's your name, anyway?" I commanded.

"Mary— What do you mean, take my clothes off? In the first place, it's cold. Secondly, it's indecent. And thirdly, you can't make me!"

"But that, my dear Mary, is the name of the game," Bert said. "I think I've seen you around school. If I remember right, you bulge out in just the right places. Let's find out. You know you can't buck this crowd." Bert gestured around at the other guys and chicks watching the scene with interest. He began to forcibly undress her. When she knew resistance was useless, she relaxed somewhat.

She got up on the slab with only a moderate amount of assistance. Some of the ritual that was leading up to the interesting part, of which she was still ignorant, even seemed to interest her mildly.

"Now, it's time for the fertility rites," I intoned. "Any of you guys who want to volunteer, stand up." Half the crowd stood up. I surmised that some of them, having gotten the drift that this chick really did not know the full story and might later charge rape, were chicken to go the full route. It did not really matter to me.

In fact, I was too doped up to try anything myself. But I would get my kicks, watching.

Then Mary got the message. She started to roll off the altar. "Hold her!" I commanded sharply.

Bert and James pinned her down fast.

A guy slipped out of his robe and came up to the altar. Mary managed to wrestle free from Bert and James. She slipped off the altar, fell to the barn's dirt floor, and crawled up to where I was sitting.

"*Please* don't!" She began to cry.

"We should have built a bigger fire," I said, sarcastically. "You're covered with goose pimples."

"You guys can't make me do *that*," Mary sobbed as Bert and James grabbed her.

"Wait, guys. Now, Mary, you are saying that you won't let us do that to you?"

"Man, that is going to be quite a hassle if she doesn't cooperate," Bert said, shaking his head and twisting her arm.

"That's right! You guys can go to hell," Mary replied.

I sighed. "I guess there's only one thing to do." I thought a minute, then said, "Okay, Bert. James. Pin her down. One of you others stomp on her hands."

Mary gasped. "Oh, God! No!"

"That's a good idea," Bert said. "She already scratched me when she was trying to get away."

Mary screamed as they pounced on her, pinning her on the floor, tummy down. Andy slipped on his heavy boots and stomped hard on her hands, grinding his heel into each hand.

She was screaming in pain.

"Okay, guys. Hold it. Mary, have you changed your mind, or do you need more convincing?"

We let her sit up, on the floor. When she could stop crying long enough, she said, "All right. Only just don't hurt me anymore!"

When it was over, the guys helped her get her clothes back on and they drove her to the doc. I made a note to double his monthly retainer that month. We had friends in the local police setup, too. I was sure that the guys taking Mary to the doc would stress this, along with our control of the demons, in persuading her to "forget it."

For the next few nights, I could not sleep, for some reason. The heroin I had taken a week ago had scared me, but at last I thought I had better try some more to see if I could get some control over my nerves. Otherwise, if I did manage to sleep, I would have haunting dreams and see all kinds of weird people, like my mother, Sister Frances . . .

I was real sick. I could not even get out of bed. "Hey, Sandy. Who was that on the phone?" I called.

"Oh, just some salesman," she replied.

"Yeah? Okay. Hey fix some more of that H. Maybe that's what I need."

"Sure, Mike," she said, coming in, smiling. "No sooner said than done."

She went to the kitchen. "Where's Carmen?" I called after her.

"Went shopping, I guess," she shouted back. She came in a moment later with the needle and some rubber tubing. "Here goes," she said, jabbing the needle into my vein.

It was not a *flash* I got this time. I got a bombardment. My muscles tightened so I could hardly move.

"What's going on?" I gasped, chewing the words out, as my jaw seemed to be frozen. "What'd you put in that . . . ?"

Sandy kind of grinned. "H. Like you said, Mike."

"How *much*?" I moaned.

She shrugged.

Everything seemed far away. Her image seemed to fade and crystallize again in waves, and her voice—I guess she was talking on the phone—drifted in and out of my consciousness.

Suddenly, there was a sea of hands around me. They were stripping my clothes off. Several arms that seemed like the backs of sharks lifted me off the bed. It must have been night, although everything was dim, anyway, and it could have been happening in floodlights. My muscles were twitching painfully, and spasm after spasm made me writhe and groan as I was carried downstairs and thrown into a car—the black Continental.

I could not tell whether I was dreaming and whether the voices I heard were real or figments of fantasy. For all I knew, the ones who threw me so roughly into the back of the car were demons.

It was dark and raining. I kept coming out of it long enough to hear the sound of cars as they passed us going the opposite direction. Voices . . .

"They said you could take over, Paul . . ."

"That's what I've been waiting for . . ."

"You going to end up blowing *your* mind . . . ?"

An evil laugh.

They were all devils. They had horns, after all. I could see them in silhouette. I felt as though I had to lean up into the air to grab enough of it into my lungs, like a fish out of water, reaching, reaching . . . My pulse was pounding and my body shaking like a Mexican jumping bean. Blinding lights seared my throbbing eyeballs, and my teeth were mangling my lips. I could feel froth and blood slathering across my chin.

The car braked to a quick stop, but the motor was still turning over. "Okay, you and you. Dump him."

I tried to raise my head, but it fell back to the seat. Darkness hit me like a force.

Chapter Eight

With Satan, everything is on a cash-and-carry basis. As long as you do for him, he will do for you. He will answer your "prayers"—if you are useful to him. He will give you what you desire. But the moment you quit giving him what *he* wants, the moment he decides you are no longer useful to him or someone else does it better—then you have had it. With Satan there is always a payback—not just when you die, but right here on earth!

I got mine in spades. My payback came when I least expected it, from the source that I could not possibly believe would do me in. Because, when I was so spaced out that I could not get out of bed to make my own fix, and I had to ask Sandy to cook it for me—well, she fixed me up, all right; she slipped me an overdose.

All those people who "loved" me and took care of me . . . who praised me . . . who patted me on the back . . . who flew me to Salem, New York, and San Francisco for conferences . . . who clothed me and provided me with a car and driver . . . who gave me money, sexual pleasures, drugs, liquor, and anything else I wanted— these same people threw me in a car, stark naked, drove me to the emergency entrance of a local hospital, and dumped me out on the pavement in the rain.

I remember coming to and seeing someone standing over me, some dude in a white coat. He kicked me in the side of the head and said, "I wonder if this guy's dead." I groaned and heard him say, "Nope! Not yet!"

When I refused to give a name and assure them I had money to pay for hospitalization, attendants gave me some first aid and bundled me off to the county hospital. There, I signed in as John Doe and was put in a huge open ward with some other dopers.

As I lay there for more than a week "drying out" in an agony of pain, during interludes of clarity, I mused about what had happened. Remembering the snatches of conversation I had overheard during occasional flashes of consciousness on that ride to the hospital, I realized I was being dumped because I was no longer maintaining my cool. Drugs and—what else could I call it?—my conscience were getting to me, and quite frankly, I was as scared as I was revolted. I guess my heart wanted to get out, even more than my ego wanted to get up. Anyway, I was no longer any good to them.

I had increased the membership of the Brotherhood from 500 to 1,500; shared valuable information with my group, information I had gleaned from Victorville and from conferences in three widely scattered regions; run thousands of dollars of dope; and jumped loyally at every command to do the bidding of Satan's agents. But now I was no good to them. There are just no second chances with Satan, no sympathy and no help when you go ape.

Most of those in the car when I was dumped were in the third stage. One was from higher up, the fourth stage. Then, there was my most trusted brother and fellow counselor, the guy who had looked after me, gotten money for me, run errands for me—Paul—the one who had now become my successor.

In Satan's "church," while you are swinging, you are Mr. Big. They come crawling to you. Lick your boots. Whatever you say is *law*. You do not even need a valid reason. You just say, "I *will* it."

But do not turn your back on them. Do not drop your guard. Do not ever falter. Because everyone wants your job. They would even kill to get it. In fact, there had been a couple of attempts on my life when I was Master Counselor. Only my shrewdness in conning the majority to be watchful on my side had allowed me to remain in power as long as I had.

But I had blown it. And now I was through. Fallen from grace. Discarded like an old shoe. I *felt* like an old shoe. I felt as if I had been worn by a roughneck kid, scuffed, kicked against rocks, shuffled, trailing my untied laces, and never polished or shined. And then chewed by the kid's big bowser while he was asleep.

For days, I could not eat. I was thirsty, but nothing seemed to quench my thirst. My muscles would not obey the commands of my brain but shuddered in painful spasms. I felt as though someone were inside my head, beating with a hammer to get out. My eyes watered, my nose ran, my flesh was on fire half the time and icy or clammy the rest of the time.

As Dr. Spitz says, "Overdoses exhibit varied symptoms." They told me mine was not a heavy overdose, nor the recovery period, eight days, very long. All that relativity talk did not make it any easier for me. It was eight days of hell. Each waking minute, a torment, and my fitful sleep charged with nightmares.

It got so bad they finally put me in an itty-bitty padded cell that they called a *rubber room,* where I beat my head against the wall until I was exhausted.

Then, fed up with the rehabilitation scene, I swiped some clothes and split for the streets. I returned to my apartment. No one was there, and many of my things were missing. The girls had probably been assigned new masters. I was alone. All alone.

There was nothing to do. The people at the hamburger joint where I had worked shook their heads. My former boss said, "You haven't worked for three weeks. You were getting pretty grouchy those last days. Then, one day, you just didn't show up. We phoned your apartment, and some girls answered and said you were busy. You never checked with us or asked for time off. You never explained what

122

the trouble was. And, now, you came back wanting to work. Huh-uh."

"But I've *got* to work."

"You didn't act as though you had to work the last few weeks you were with us," the boss continued. "You acted like you were doing us a favor. Then you didn't show up at all. What were we supposed to do, tell our customers they'd have to come back later?" He shook his head. "We have to have dependable people, Mike. Besides, just look at you . . ."

Thus, without friends to pass the time with, afraid to show up at college for fear of bumping into guys who were still in the organization, and without a job to keep me occupied, I had nothing to distract me from my thoughts. I was trapped on the endless carrousel of my mind.

In the hospital, I had suffered. Now I was suffering in a different way, suffering for what I had done to others. I didn't believe I had any conscience left. In fact, in the Brotherhood, any reference to conscience was the equivalent of a dirty joke.

But I did have one, after all—a conscience with a capital C. And as bad as it was now making me feel, deep down I was grateful that I still *could* feel bad; I'd met too many guys who would never feel anything again.

I thought back on those whom I had caused to suffer in some degree or other. I had been like those creeps who had dumped me. At last I could appreciate what I had done to others.

Still, it did not stop me from going back to smoking pot and shooting speed. I had been psychologically habituated to both and physically addicted to the speed, and eight days of cold turkey in the ward had not diminished my craving. My body ached for it.

I had had it with Satan, and I was mad at God. I blamed Him for letting me get myself into this mess and then not doing anything to help me. Not that I had ever asked Him. Nor was I about to ask Him now. No one would ever see Mike Warnke begging for help!

123

So there I sat, alone with my conscience. Its voice was neither still nor small; it came on loud and clear, frequently shouting at me day and night. I could not really rest, yet I lacked the strength or confidence to do anything worthwhile.

I wanted to go home, but how could I explain being out of work, out of money, out of tune, a mental and physical wreck? If I told my mother I had been in witchcraft and was on drugs, it would kill her.

I was too ashamed to see my parents. I was ashamed to see anyone I had known when I was straight, and I was too bitter—and afraid—to try to re-make the scene with my recent "friends." When you fall out of favor with those guys, you fall a long way out.

The rule of the game was, the bigger you are, the harder you fall. A little guy might be invited to come back, later, after he had learned his lesson. Not me.

Also, they might have cause to worry about a little guy who had not really become all that involved yet. Despite their threats, he just might talk. If they did not have much of a hold over him, it would be better to have him *in*, where they could get him more involved and watch him closely. But they had too much on me. And the cops knew all about it, too. If I spilled my guts, they could get me put away for years. And I didn't dare even *think* about what they might have their demons do to me. The unspoken deal was understood to be, "Me no talkee, they no talkee."

Alone with my conscience, I knew no pleasures in life, no satisfactions—and no hope.

Finally, I couldn't bear it any longer; I had to call home. At least on the phone they could not see me. "I'm *okay*, Mom," I said, after we had greeted one another. "No, I'm not in college. I dropped out. No, I don't have a job. No, I can't come over right now. Please, Mom, you've got to stop crying." I was beginning to cry myself, something I hadn't done in years.

"You see, I've got some—interviews—coming up. I have to go—yeah, job interviews. That's it. Where? To—um—San Diego for a few days. I have to leave right away.

Oh, yeah, the Navy. That's right, I'm really considering that."

It wasn't entirely a lie. Three months earlier I had seen a recruiter on a quirk and had actually filled out much of the paperwork. I didn't know why I had said San Diego, but Mom had picked up on it, and the Navy just might be the out I was looking for.

Somehow, I was able to terminate the conversation gently, but afterward I was shot, really a mess.

In order to eat and get my supplies of speed, I had had to start selling a few of my "dollies and dishes." I also chanced a little pushing. But it was a hassle, because the people I bought the stuff from were up-and-coming first- and second-stagers in the very organization which had ousted me.

I was not sure whether these jokers who were "working their way through college" and up in the organization knew who I was, but anyway, they were charging plenty for their merchandise. I could hardly, on the other hand, go to my former friends in the third-stage and ask for my former discount. "Hi, guys. We've had a bit of a tiff, but let's let bygones be bygones. Can't we have business as usual?"

It was hard peddling my personal effects, and I had to let stuff go for a fraction of its value. I knew that once everything was sold that I intended to sell, I would really be sweating it.

I could not go home, and I could not go back. The only thing to do was to get away, as far away as possible. So, this Navy deal seemed a definite answer.

I had another long talk with the naval recruiter in the San Bernardino post-office building, and he thought we could get a waiver on my police record, particularly since I had not actually been convicted of anything except traffic violations. The old fixaroo had helped me there.

The recruiter was so confident, he told me to be ready to catch a bus the moment my papers came through. It was 1966, and our commitment in Vietnam had surpassed the number of men we had in Korea at the height of that war. I guess he thought they needed me.

During the next few days, *my* confidence in making it dwindled to a big fat zero. They would not have me, a virtual speed freak, a guy with a police record in several cities, even if I had not actually had to appear in court. A guy like me? I did not have a single reference.

Finally I decided to take a chance and see what the campus at Valley College was like now. I went over there on the bus. I was walking around the campus, and suddenly I saw this chick coming toward me. I froze. It was Mary, the girl we had kidnapped and—I didn't want to think about it.

Then another thought struck me: Man, if she knew I had been kicked out of the Brotherhood and did not have my protection anymore . . . I was scared. I started moving, businesslike, in another direction.

She saw me! She came up and said, "I know you."

"Yeah. I know you, too. So what?" I kept walking. Put on a big front, play indifferent. She walked beside me till I stopped and said, "What do you want, precisely?"

She smiled. She actually smiled, the girl I had told the guys to grab off the street, strip, stomp, and rape. That smile hurt more than anything my conscience had said in the past three weeks. She said, "I don't want anything. I just came over to tell you I love you."

"You *what?*" Had what had happened to her blown her mind? Was she some kind of happy vegetable? I wanted to run. Hide. Die.

"I said, I love you. I've accepted Jesus as my Savior. And I love you."

She was sane. More than that, she was beautiful—shining with a radiance that was beyond the sun's.

"I, uh—" It was too much for me. Just too much. I turned and split—just like that—leaving her standing under the trees.

The experience completely shattered me. I was too stubborn to admit that God had anything for me—too full of sin, in any case, to believe that He would accept me.

And when I thought of all the things I had deliberately done to blaspheme and defile Him . . . I had nothing to offer Him, no way to buy His favor. So, what was all this *love* junk about? The girl was just plain nuts. That was the only explanation. Jesus care? No one cared, not about Mike Warnke.

It got under my skin, nevertheless—as bad as speed ever had. That *word!* The wanting to believe that it was more than just a word, yet the doubt and my self-condemnation telling me that I did not deserve to be loved —or to love. It really bugged me. I was climbing the walls. *Love! A lie!* And I sank into the blackest depression of my life.

I had forty-five dollars left. The thought came into my head to spend it in the most productive way I could think of. I took a walk in the shoddy part of town, dipped into a couple of gun shops, then a pawnshop I knew from witchcraft days, where the guy sold weapons and ammo, no questions asked and no registration required. There I found what I was looking for, a good gun, a .38 caliber Smith & Wesson snub-nose. The gun and one bullet came to $44.98. One bullet would be more than enough.

Outside on the sidewalk, the sun reflected off of something shiny—a quarter. "Leave it," the thought came. "Get on with it." No, it was just enough for a cup of coffee, and I headed back to the campus student union to buy it.

I would not need anything else. Ever.

At the student union, I got my coffee and settled myself at a table away from normal union traffic to prepare for the big sacrifice—my last! With my hands under the table, I checked the gun over, loaded it, and put it back into my pocket. I had just started composing a note, when some student evangelists from Campus Crusade happened to pass by.

Their happiness was overflowing as they strolled in a small group singing, "His name is wonderful . . . Jesus, my Lord. He is the mighty King, Master of everything, His name is wonderful, Jesus, my Lord. He's the great

127

Shepherd, the Rock of all ages, almighty God is He. Bow down before Him. Love and adore Him. His name is wonderful, Jesus my Lord."

What *right* did they have to be so happy? Then the thought came that they were singing deliberately to taunt me. They were celebrating my demise. Joyous at the prospect of reading my obituary. Damn them all anyway!

Well, I would show them. And Satan. And God, too. I would *not* kill myself, after all. I would live and let my life be a goad to all of them.

I threw the gun in the apartment manager's trash can . . . And that was the end of that.

Now that I had decided to live, the only thing to do was to join the Navy and see the world. I had seen hell already.

Training was another not-so-merry-go-round, and sick as I was, it really slaughtered me. I was still kicking the drug thing and having all the pain from that heaped on the rigorous training schedule—up at dawn, running around all morning; and after lunch, sitting down only for lectures, and pulling some kind of duty. No time off while we were in boot camp. No visitors. Just work, work, work! I got fire watch every third day—or, rather, night—walk around the barracks to see that nothing burned up, dead tired from a stiff workout during the day, angry at the world I had once looked forward to the seeing.

The first thing I had heard when I stumbled off the bus at the disassembly point, or whatever they called it, was, "Hey, you! Boy. You, hippie! Come over here. Put your toes on that line and stand still."

He was talking to *me*. I turned around to get back on the bus! But the driver had closed the door and was starting off.

I jumped, ran to the line. That barrel-chested Chief scared the pants off me. I do not know why. Maybe it was his voice. It was gruff, tinged with sarcasm. His face showed he knew where he was going, and no one was going to stand in his way.

A couple groups of sailors walked by our area of confused recruits. "You'll be sorry!" they jeered.

I was sorry already.

We were forced into a semblance of a line and harangued and insulted. Between insults, we were told the rules of the game, what dire misfortunes were going to happen to us for the next trillion years, how the Chief and all others concerned with our training were going to make us shape up even if it killed us, how it was a shame to waste all that good chow on a bunch of dumb-johns . . . The Chief walked up and down the line, taking in every aspect of his new crew and shaking his head. It almost seemed that he was crying with the shame of it—"Who the devil was in charge of you guys' recruiting posts?" he said, incredulously.

After he dismissed us in the charge of another petty officer, who was told to *march* us to our "place of confinement," he caught up with us again as we were desperately trying to keep in step.

"You, hippie! I'm coming to the barracks," he yelled at me, "as soon as you've stowed your gear, and I'm going to *personally* escort you to our first-class barber." Someone laughed, and he whirled on him. "That means you, too. All you punks. You're all going to get regulation white-walls, even if we have to tie you to the chair. The barber don't like people wiggling in the chair, and he's got sharp scissors, so if you want to keep your worthless ears on your head, you better shape up when he's operating."

That Chief still had it in for me, because when he marched us over to the barber's, he stood by the barber's shoulder the whole time that butcher was mangling my beautiful long hair and personally instructed the barber what to do and how to do it.

The Chief kept holding on to *one* particular strand of hair. "Cut around that, mate," he told the barber in a tone slightly more kindly than he had used with us. "We'll just *save* that one to remind him of this occasion forever." He tilted my chin up with his hand, almost making the barber nip an ear. "And, you, hippie—you better not let that one hair get 'lost.' When Clem, here is through with you, you ask him for some tape and you tape that hair down when you're sleeping, just so it don't get lost. You hear that squirrel!"

"How can I?" I murmured. "He just amputated one ear and you blew the eardrum out of the other."

"Oh, you're still a smart punk, eh? Wait a while. You'll get the message and good." He stalked off to wait outside and watch some waves rippling along.

When the barber got through with me, he gave the chair a whirl that sent me flying out and almost landing on my face. He had buzzed me right down to the scalp! I was looking bad enough to begin with, but now I looked like a zombie. And that one hair stayed with me throughout bootcamp.

And to top it all off—talk about rotten luck—of the eighty-five guys in our outfit, there were two who believed in Jesus Christ, and guess what their last names were. Wardel and Washburn—which meant that I got stuck with *both* of them for roommates. I mean, of all the lousy coincidences!

They really got me furious, all the time spouting off about Jesus. I got in violent arguments with them. "What's all this Jesus stuff doing for you, mates?" I would ask. "Sure, it might be all right for the hereafter, but what about the here-and-now? What are you going to be, meek and mild and have other people stomp on you? Turn the other cheek and get that one clobbered, too?"

"The trouble with you and a lot of other people," Bill Wardel said, "is that you don't see Jesus as a real person. But He *is* a person, Mike."

"Yeah," Bob Washburn agreed. "He's not remote, off at the end of the universe somewhere. You can get to know Him and talk with Him, just like we're talking right now."

I shook my head. "*Your* trouble," I retorted, "is having a super-big imagination."

But I well knew, from the past I was trying to forget, just how real Satan was. It stood to reason his arch-adversary was equally real. And according to them, He had a whole lot more power, but power that manifested itself in love, not hate. I began to listen to them more carefully, although I would not admit it. Listened more and questioned less. I even let them drag me to church once. The chapel on the base was blah. I could not understand how Bob and Bill got anything out of it, but they did. "Jesus is there, even if you don't care for the chaplain," they tried to explain.

But I kept dragging them over the coals. My stubborn streak kept me from really understanding what they were saying.

However, the fact that they helped me—instinctively, repeatedly, when I really needed it—got to me. While I was still kicking the speed habit, I would wake up at night with cold sweats and be too sick to get out of my bunk. My body was racked with aches and pains, my stomach threatening to explode its contents, my muscles twitching. They would cover me with their dry blankets, hanging the sweaty ones up to dry—and then sleep without blankets themselves! They would get up in the middle of the night to get me a drink of water when my throat was burning like fire.

One night, I was walking around the barracks on fire watch, feeling miserable, the clammy chills and queasy stomach adding to my mood. I walked my post, looking into the various cubicles where the guys slept.

Most of the fellows lay in their racks in restless sleep, tossing and turning, crying out occasionally, muttering and gnashing their teeth. They were not getting much rest, despite the fact they had arisen early the previous morning and might, at any time, be routed out of bed for a surprise hike, a surprise "lesson," or just a surprise inspection—all of it done to condition us to the unexpected.

All were restless except the two Christians. They were sleeping peacefully, like babies. I caught my breath; there was a radiance about their faces. It was *real*—a visible thing. They were positively *glowing!*

It really got to me, so I went outside and watched the lights on the water. A jet had just roared across the sky, its sound splitting the quiet, leaving a trail in the night. But it was quiet again now, and the stars were winking. The moon was low, near the water-line, about to sink— full, golden, the face on it smiling sadly. The water was calm, and the shadow of a destroyer made a black swath across the field of diffused lights which the city had washed into the water. The scene made me feel nostalgic, homesick. I got a soft, mushy feeling.

It was hard to tell in what direction my emotion would go from there. Usually it soured into bitterness, anger, and ultimately violent hatred, sometimes for some definite person in my life who had, I thought, shafted me. But mostly the rage would be directed against something or someone intangible and abstract, which was even more frustrating.

I turned back to the barracks and, my jaw clenched, wandered through the building. I paused by the center-board, a table which ran the length of the barracks and was used for studying and letter-writing. On it lay something that belonged to Bill Wardel, who was in the habit of writing to his girl friend every evening. Since she was a Christian, too, he would use his Bible to find verses of Scripture to quote. It was his Bible he had left on the table —open.

Chapter Nine

The Bible lay face down on the table, next to his writing pad. "I'd better put that in the cube," I thought. "He could get in trouble for leaving personal effects lying around if the Chief called an inspection."

When I picked it up to put it away, curiosity made me look to see where it was open. John 3:16 was underlined, and my eyes were revited to that verse. *For God so loved the world, that he gave his only begotten Son, that whosoever believeth in him should not perish, but have everlasting life.*

I read on, trying to figure out why this page had been left open. Both he and his girl were Christians, and they would surely have known this Scripture by heart. Anyhow, the "why" behind the situation puzzled me. Just from reading this one verse, I felt emotionally moved—an all-choked-up feeling.

I stood there thinking about how Bob and Bill had been so concerned about me for the past few weeks. Why? I had not shown them any consideration, only arguments, a sharp tongue, taunts, and ridicule. A lump was building up in my throat as I pondered these things.

Then I thought about how these two guys seemed to be blessed with something special, something the other guys in the barracks did not have—peace. And love.

I don't know how long I stood there, my eyes filling with tears so I could no longer see the page. This was it, I realized. The end of the line. There was nothing left to say, nowhere else to go. The only answer was to be sought on my knees. As a tough guy, I had tried everything else —sex, drugs, witchcraft, and Satanism. Why not talk to God? I certainly had nothing left.

I looked around the barracks. It was not private enough for what I wanted to say, and the last thing I wanted was to be overheard. I spotted the mop closet at the end of the barracks, and taking the Bible with me, went in and shut the door. There, kneeling alongside dirty mops, with my arms resting on a mop bucket, clutching the Bible, I began to pray. Tears streamed down my cheeks.

"Hey, God," I sobbed, "I never did this before. But I'm willing to trust You, Lord. I don't know if I have the right to talk to You—it seems strange to turn to You now, after . . . everything. Well, I'm ready to put my life into Your hands. I believe what Bob and Bill told me about Your power, and I see it says the same thing in Your Book. It also says that You will forgive me for all my sins. I have a hard time believing that, God. But if that's true, I'm willing to give them to You and be cleaned up inside. Lord, I've got a lot of sins to confess, but I know You got time to listen . . ."

I knelt there for about two hours, turning all my sins over to God—naming each sin that I could remember. I prayed about witchcraft. I prayed about Satanism. I prayed about Mary. I prayed about everything. As I prayed, I felt a tremendous physical burden lift from me as if it were some heavy weight, and a feeling of unbelievable peacefulness came over me.

This was something I had never felt before, not even when I had gone to the church when I was smaller. This was different. This was not the "awestruck kid that was gone on ritual." I thought back to those days and wondered why I had not seen the real meaning then. I finally got up and went back out into the barracks, sat down, and started thumbing through the Bible.

I read the Sermon on the Mount for the first time.

Blessed are the poor in spirit: for theirs is the kingdom of heaven.

Blessed are they that mourn: for they shall be comforted.

Blessed are the meek: for they shall inherit the earth.

Blessed are they which do hunger and thirst after righteousness: for they shall be filled.

Blessed are the merciful: for they shall obtain mercy.

Blessed are the pure in heart: for they shall see God.

Some of the verses bothered me, like the ones about being merciful and pure of heart. I wondered if God really *could* find it in His heart to forgive *all* the things I had done. I read the entire Gospel of John and received still further assurance that I was indeed saved. It almost seemed as if the Bible was turning the pages itself, turning to places that I should read. I could not put it down. I stayed up long after my relief assumed the watch, until the sun rose, not even bothering to get into the sack. When Bob and Bill got up and came over to greet me, I was grinning from ear to ear.

"What's with you? You look like you got a good night's sleep for a change," Bob said.

I grinned and pointed to the Bible. "I've been sitting up all night reading and trying to understand what you guys have been telling me. It finally got through to me, and—I took Jesus into my heart!"

"Hallelujah!" Bob shouted, waking anyone in the barracks who might still be sleeping. Bill started jumping around, and Bob hit me on the back so hard I thought I was going to choke. They went wild with joy, and the three of us raced around the barracks like a bunch of nuts. The other fellows that were still in the sack thought we were crazy, rolled over, and put pillows over their heads.

Finally exhausted, we just collapsed at one end of my bunk, hugging and slapping each other on the back with pure joy.

Now committed, I was determined to do my best for the Lord. From then on, every time I had a free minute, even

135

while shining my shoes, Bob and Bill would come up to me and say, "Hey, we found some interesting Scripture you might like to read." They gave me the Bible opened to Matthew 7. "Look at verse 13, Mike," Bob said.

Enter ye in at the strait gate: for wide is the gate, and broad is the way, that leadeth to destruction, and many there be which go in thereat.

"I think verse 14 might also help, Mike," Bill said.

I had to go on reading, as I did not know these verses, or hardly any of the Bible for that matter. *Because strait is the gate, and narrow is the way, which leadeth unto life, and few there be that find it.*

I looked back at the guys who were putting the shoe polish away for me. "Yeah, I see what you mean. I'm just glad it isn't too late for me."

While waiting in line for chow, I noticed a change in myself that was already hard to believe. The old, arrogant, push-to-the-front Mike was gone. I did not even mind waiting in lines any longer, nor did I expect anyone to move aside for me. Even my voice was softer. I did not yell anymore, just talked in an ordinary voice, and people heard me.

I did not have to prove to anyone that I was a big guy or a hard guy anymore, although the rest of the guys still liked to tease and call me hippie. Even the Chief's attitude seemed to change toward me.

Boot camp finally ended, and we were all granted a two-week leave. There was a special feeling of gladness in me now. I was going home for the first time in almost a year, looking forward to seeing my parents, eager to show them I had become a human being again. I had invited Gene, another friend from boot camp, to come home with me.

We stopped off at the apartment of a friend to see if he was okay and if the personal effects I had left with him were all right.

"I dunno what happened, Mike," he said. "I was out of town for a while, and when I got back and checked, all your boxes were gone except a few, and they had been opened and books strewn all over. I packed them back in, but there isn't much left." The poor guy looked so helpless, probably waiting for me to smash him one, like I might have done before.

"Well, aren't you going to punch me out?"

"Why should I?" I held out my hand to show him there were no hard feelings. "You can't fight those guys." Looking back out front I saw his car. "Would you mind driving us over to Jake's place to see about my other stuff? All the heavy pieces are still there, like the couch, chair, stereo, and coffee table. Guess I had better get it out of his way before it gets ruined."

"Sure, glad to be of some help," he said, probably still puzzled at the change in me.

On the way over, I explained what had been happening to me in boot camp and that I was completely out of witchcraft. I told him about my plans for the future with God on my side now.

"Just wait till your folks hear about this! It'll be hard for them to believe." We both looked at each other shyly, remembering the fights we had had, me being the tough guy.

"If you want to go on up to Crestline after we get through at Jake's, I have nothing better to do. I'll drive you on up." I mumbled my thanks, wondering why I had not seen how nice a guy he was before.

Jake's place looked the same—still the neat appearance and the well-kept lawn. We looked around and finally found him out in back, pulling weeds.

"Mike! Glad to see ya," Jake said, putting his arm on my shoulder. "I thought maybe you had taken off for parts unknown. In fact, with that new 'hairdo' I wasn't sure who it was for a minute."

"The Navy has ways of changing people," I said. "How about letting me get my stuff off of your hands? I surely appreciate your keeping it for me."

"Hey, man, I thought you had your stuff." Jake

frowned. "You didn't let me know you were leaving, and then someone came to collect all of your furniture one night when I was out. I just figured it was you, or you had sent some of those 'friends' of yours."

"Wasn't any of your stuff ripped off?" I asked.

"Nope, not a thing of mine was taken. I'm sorry." Embarrassed, he turned back to his weeding, and I could see that it was pointless to ask any more questions. "Well, thanks for keeping it as long as you did, Jake. We'll be shoving off." I signaled to Gene and my friend to head out.

On the way up to Crestline, I started thinking about the possessions that I had been worried about—the china, books, furniture, clothes. It was all gone now! I owned just what I had in my duffel bag. I started to laugh.

"What's so funny?" Gene asked. He probably thought I had flipped.

"I guess it isn't really *funny*, but this is one way the Lord has taught me a lesson. Those were all things Satan had provided for me. I guess it's poetic justice."

Homecoming was all that I'd hoped it would be and then some. In all, I spent two weeks at home. We had all our meals together without arguments, and for the first time my brother and I were not hassling each other. In fact, he seemed proud to take me to see his friends, and we bummed around the area together for the first time in years.

Just for something to do, I went to the grocery store for Mom, and while I was pushing the cart past the produce section, I noticed two girls standing there. Their baskets were half full, and I had to move one to get by them.

"Mike? Mike Warnke?" one of the girls asked.

I turned around and was surprised to see Sue Studer, the girl who had always dated the football heroes. Sue was still as pretty as ever, and the girl she had with her was another old school acquaintance named Ruth Lundy. It was great to see them again.

After talking to the girls awhile, catching up on the news, I said, "Say, why don't my buddy and I take you two to see *The Ten Commandments* at the movie? Have you seen it yet?"

"No, I haven't. Ruth, have you?" Sue asked, and Ruth shook her head indicating she had not seen it either.

I made arrangements to pick up the girls, and we finished our shopping. I was surprised to see that the store had not changed much—you still had to hunt for things just like in a small store. I had thought they would have a big new supermarket up here by now.

It did not take much persuading to talk my buddy Gene into meeting the girls and taking them to the movie. Afterward, while we were having coffee and dessert at one of the local hangouts, I told them about my long battle in coming to terms with Jesus Christ.

"Oh, Mike, that's wonderful," Sue said, and Ruth beamed. "I knew something was different about you. You just can't imagine how happy I am for you. You know, I accepted the Lord in 1965." She bubbled on about how she and her friends used to pray for me.

"You know, that's hard to believe. Why would you waste your time worrying about me? I was such a creep compared to the guys you were going out with." After the waitress refilled our cups for the fourth time, we decided to leave.

"Will you come down and see us before school starts again?" Sue asked. "I'm going to be rooming with two other girls. Here, I'll write down our address and the directions to our place."

I did not want to tell her how well I knew that area. In fact, that was one of the places the guy used to pick up stray cats for our rituals. I could see that my past was not going to leave me right away. If I wanted to see the girls, I was going to have to risk running into some of the "group" in San Bernardino.

Later that night, I got down on my knees and prayed that Sue and her new roommates would be able to accept the story I was going to have to tell them. I prayed for the Lord to lead me to more Christians. I knew I had a long road ahead of me, and I was going to need help. The fact

139

that Sue and her new roommates were Christians and seemed to want to see me again was encouraging. Sue had told me that one of her roommates was another high-school acquaintance named Lorrie, who had accepted Christ, too. I knew they would be the right influence for me, as well as being fun to be around.

Before I left boot camp, I had decided to go on to Hospital Corps School and train to be a medic, thinking I could be of more use to God mending guys than swabbing decks. I was assured that I would not have to carry weapons if I was sent overseas.

Getting back to the base was not so bad now; being out of boot camp was at least one step up, and in school we were kept busy. Every time I got liberty, I headed back to see Lorrie and Sue. I started going with Lorrie, but if Sue did not have a date, we would ask her to go along, and the three of us became very close. In our dates around town, we started running into people I had known on campus before, and word soon got around that I had become a Christian. By this time I had told the girls all of the gory details of being connected with the Brotherhood.

All of a sudden, I started getting letters from Carmen, one of the girls who had lived with me before, begging me to come back to the Brotherhood and offering all kinds of lures, promising that I would not get dumped again. The fellow that had taken my place was okay, but he was not pulling in the members that I had. At first I could not figure out why they had suddenly taken such an interest in me. Then it dawned on me: since I had become a Christian, they were afraid I would talk. More than that, they would know that I was not afraid of them anymore.

Sue had worked on the staff of Campus Crusade for Christ at the Arrowhead Springs Headquarters, and her grounding in the Bible was a tremendous help to me. Whenever I would become discouraged at the depressing and embarrassing letters Carmen kept writing to me, Sue would give me passages from the Bible to read which would inspire me to keep going. One day she opened the

Bible to Psalm ninety-one, and asked me to read it out loud to her.

He that dwelleth in the secret place of the most High shall abide under the shadow of the Almighty. I will say of the Lord, He is my refuge and my fortress: my God; in him will I trust. Surely he shall deliver thee from the snare of the fowler, and from the noisome pestilence. He shall cover thee with his feathers, and under his wings shalt thou trust: his truth shall be thy shield and buckler. Thou shalt not be afraid for the terror by night; nor for the arrow that flieth by day; Nor for the pestilence that walketh in darkness; nor for the destruction that wasteth at noonday. A thousand shall fall at thy side, and ten thousand at thy right hand; but it shall not come nigh thee. Only with thine eyes shalt thou behold and see the reward of the wicked. Because thou hast made the Lord, which is my refuge, even the most High, thy habitation; There shall no evil befall thee, neither shall any plague come nigh thy dwelling. For he shall give his angels charge over thee, to keep thee in all thy ways. They shall bear thee up in their hands, lest thou dash thy foot against a stone. Thou shalt tread upon the lion and adder: the young lion and the dragon shalt thou trample under feet. Because he hath set his love upon me, therefore will I deliver him: I will set him on high, because he hath known my name. He shall call upon me, and I will answer him: I will be with him in trouble; I will deliver him, and honour him. With long life will I satisfy him, and shew him my salvation.

Then she asked me to get down on my knees and pray with her. She had such confidence, she just would not give up. In order to counteract Carmen's letters, which were now turning into threats, Sue began writing to me every day at corps school, suggesting Scriptures that I should read. I was beginning to suspect someone was prompting Carmen to keep the letters up, and I soon found out I was right.

I began to worry about the girls living alone in a trailer

park. Like most trailer parks, this one had a lot of retired couples who did not want to be bothered, nor would they be of much help in case someone tried to get at the girls. I warned them about going out alone at night, but they did not seem to think anyone or anything could possibly harm them.

Next, I got a strange letter from my mother telling me that someone named Charlotte had paid her a visit, demanding a book on voodoo or something.

"Mike, this rough-looking girl asked me, 'Where is the book? We know you must have it.' I never did think much of your old friends, and I don't appreciate them coming around here like they owned the place. Were those your friends from school?

"Your Dad showed them the door in no uncertain terms. I hope they don't show up here again, because your father means business."

At first when I read the letter I was scared. Then I got out one of Sue's letters and found some Scripture that helped. I was determined not to let these things get me down, and I had enough faith in God by now to know that Satan could not get his hands on me again. But what about Lorrie, Sue, my parents, and my friends? I remembered what the Brotherhood had done to the professor's children—the car accident—and shuddered. Before I left on liberty for the weeknd, I tucked Mom's letter in my bag, determined to show it to Lorrie and Sue and warn them again about what this crowd was capable of doing.

Before I could even get out of the taxi Saturday morning, after it pulled into the trailer park, Lorrie was sputtering something about an accident that had happened to Sue. I got out and raced into the trailer, thinking the worst.

Sue was sitting on the couch when I came in, looking radiant as usual, but slightly pale. I think she was shaken more than she cared to admit. Her left leg was bandaged halfway to her knee, and she had it propped on a footstool. My concern for her must have shown. Before I could ask any questions, she began to explain.

"It's nothing, Mike. Just a sprained ankle. I can't even explain how it happened for sure. We were in gym class, just going in for our showers—"

I sat down beside her and took hold of her hand. She went on. "I didn't see anything on the steps that I could have tripped on, so I must have missed a step. Anyhow, I fell and sprained my ankle. Two girls helped me get to a place where I could sit down. Someone else gave me a towel to wrap around my ankle and helped me to the first aid room.

"This girl that was right behind me kept watching me and saying how sorry she was, like she had made me trip or something." Sue thought for a minute, then said, "I think I've seen her around campus before. Her name is Charlotte, or something like that."

"Charlotte?"

"I guess so, I'm not sure. She was a tall blonde girl," she said, turning to Lorrie to see if she was right.

"Yes, I've seen her many times, but I can't figure out what she was doing in our gym class. She is in another section, I'm sure."

I put my head in my hands and let out a groan. "That figures." I pulled out the letter from my mother and let them read it. "I'm afraid this is just the beginning of Satan's work and the work of his demons. You couldn't know this, but Charlotte is one of the top gals in the Brotherhood. She probably put Carmen up to writing those letters, which I've burned."

"The only thing for us to do is pray harder, Mike," Sue said. "If we let these people think that we fear them, we're lost."

"I'll agree to that, but you girls are going to have to move. I had already made up my mind to that before I got that letter from Mom. Now this . . ." I took Sue's hand in mine again. "If anything should happen to you, because of my past . . ."

Suddenly Lorrie got up. "I've got something to check on. I'll be back later when you two have decided what to do." Without waiting for an answer, she bolted out the door.

In my concern over Sue, my true feelings had surfaced, and Lorrie had seen it before we had. Even I was surprised at the tremendous feeling that came over me for Sue.

She spent the next weekend in San Diego at the Hanalei Hotel, not far from the naval base. While she was there, we went to see *Dr. Zhivago,* and I quickly forgot about discussing the girls' moving plans and got wrapped up in the love story, the theme song—"Somewhere My Love"—sticking in my mind.

As the movie progressed over the snow-covered hillsides and through the valleys of daisies and daffodils, I realized my love was not "somewhere," but right beside me. I was not sure whether to let it out or not, but I put my arm around Sue and she snuggled up close.

"Mike, don't look so serious. This is supposed to be a happy time, when two people find out they love each other. With the Lord on our side, we can't lose. Look how far He has brought you already, leading you to me."

"Yes, but what are you getting?" I asked. "I can't even offer you safety right now." There were so many promises I wanted to make to her, I thought, as people began leaving the theater. "I can't even predict what might happen to all of us. Did Lorrie know how we felt about each other before this?"

"I think she had known for quite some time, Mike. She was the one who encouraged me to write to you, saying she was too busy." We sat there for some time, not even talking, just glad to be together. Where was the smooth-tongued orator now? I was in the midst of one of the most important moments of my life, and I could not even get the right words out. By this time, the usher was giving us the eye, and we noticed we were the only people remaining in the theater.

"When would you like to get married?" I finally blurted out as we waited outside the theater for a taxi.

Usually, Sue was not at a loss for words either. Finally

she said, "We'll have to let you get through school first, and find out how the Navy looks on this. I can stay with Lorrie until we get married. I haven't even started to major in anything yet; I've just been taking prerequisites."

"While we're waiting, I wish you could be closer."

"You can call me often, and we'll see each other almost every weekend," Sue reminded me. "I'm not afraid, Mike, if that's what you're worried about."

The next day I telephoned my mother to tell her of our marriage plans.

"What's a nice girl like Sue marrying you for? I hope you really mean what you say about changing, Mike. It's not fair to her if you aren't going to stick by her. Have you set a date yet?"

"No, Mom. We talked about it for the first time last night. I have to finish Hospital Corps School first, and I want to know where I'll be sent and if she can go with me."

"Does she know about your 'old friends'?" Mom asked.

"Yes, but she isn't afraid. With Jesus to cling to, I'm sure we'll make it."

"Well, you have always made up your own mind about everything, anyway. Just be sure and let us know when you plan to get married." She paused, thinking about what to say next. "Marriage is serious, Mike, and should be for a lifetime."

The next few days were hectic. The girls found a place to move and decided it would be best to move at night so they would not be seen and no one would know where they had gone. They might as well have moved in the daylight, though, because they were followed by two bats, everywhere they went.

After they were moved in and settled, I noticed there was a big black cat that kept hanging around outside the front gate. It gave me the creeps every time I went by, and I did not tell the girls I thought it was a demon, too. They already know about the bats.

I tried to keep my mind on my studies, and calling Sue every night helped. She never had a negative thought and kept encouraging me to read as much in the Bible as possible, so I would be able to fight oppression.

With Sue's love to back me up, I began to trust the Lord more and more. One weekend when I was visiting Sue, I pulled into the parking lot of a local supermarket and ran straight into Charlotte. I was going in the door, and she was coming out—crash. She took one look at me and ran to her car, got in, and split. Now *she* was the one who was afraid. I was beginning to feel the Lord was on my side after all. I was really encouraged until one night a week later, when I called Sue.

After our usual greeting she said, "Guess what happened to Lorrie? I knew you warned her not to, but she kept on playing detective on those witchcraft people."

"Sue! What happened?"

"She got shot at outside a warehouse, trying to get some license numbers. It was at one of the night meetings of the Brotherhood. She told me she was actually going to go in, but when she got to the door, someone knew she wasn't one of the group. She turned and ran back to her car, and just after she got in and started to drive off, someone shot at her."

"Is she all right? Did she report it to the police?" I asked.

"Yes. I don't know why she went alone. Usually her friend goes with her. They are both interested in finding out all they can about this group."

"I hope you've been thinking of a date to get married," I said, changing the subject. "I'll be through school soon, and there is no reason why we can't get married and be together, away from all of the worry with you up there and me down here."

"I'm ready anytime you say, darling. How about May thirteenth? Give me a couple of weeks to check on the date. I'll let you know when you call tomorrow night."

Between Sue and Jesus, I had something to hang onto now, some direction and purpose to my life.

But a week later, my warnings to the girls about being careful were fulfilled in a big way in my own life. It was almost dark, and I was over near the college, walking along the street toward Sue's apartment. I had been leaving my car in different places, hoping my movements would not be obvious. I was dreaming about Sue, not paying any attention to people or cars going by. Suddenly there was a *whinging* shot and a dull *whap*. A huge Cadillac, which had evidently been cruising slowly by, tooled off with a deafening roar. I looked around and saw I was standing near a telephone pole and there was a faint wisp of haze dissipating from a neat little hole. I looked closely and saw that there was a .22 caliber slug embedded about a quarter of an inch deep in the telephone pole. I ran the rest of the way to Sue's apartment.

My would-be assassins were either lousy shots, or the Lord deflected their aim. I decided not to report it to the police. I did not want them digging into my background.

"Mike!" Sue exclaimed, taking one look at me.

"Turn out the lights, and let's sit over here away from the window," I said, flicking the wall switch as Sue went for the table lamp.

We sat on the couch. "Same old trick they played on Lorrie. I wish you wouldn't stay here by yourself. Couldn't the girls have waited until I got here, before they took off?"

Sue squeezed my hand. "Mike, you worry too much. If I'm going to start being afraid of my own shadow, we might as well give up."

"I just don't want anyone taking a shot at you, too, Sue." I kissed her tenderly, aware of what a precious gift God had given me and how utterly lost, alone, and unhappy I would be if anything should happen to her.

On my next visit to Sue's everything seemed to be going well, when suddenly I felt as though sharp fingers were gripping at my shoulders and shoving.

My brain kind of whirled—that's the only way I can describe it—and I felt as if my mind had suddenly detached itself from my head and was up in a corner of the room, looking down on my body—suddenly no longer being in

147

control of it. My body got up and stumbled halfway across the room to where Sue was sitting by the telephone table. My hands reached out, and my fingers grasped the cross she wore around her neck and pulled. The chain on which the cross had dangled snapped, and I let it slip through my fingers as they curled around her throat.

"Mike! *Mike!*" Sue screamed, throwing her arms up and trying to grab my arms, at the same time twisting and trying to get up out of the chair. "Mike! Stop it!" She grabbed my wrist and held on. "Jesus! Release Mike from these demons. Help us, Jesus."

As soon as she said Jesus' name, I let go. I felt my mind descending back into my head, and control tingling through my muscles. I dropped my arms and stood back and looked at Sue. "Oh, God! Forgive me!" I took her in my arms. We were both shaking like we had caught hold of a jackhammer handle. "Do you see why I keep worrying about what Satan can still do to me?" I shook my head. Later we prayed together, and I went home.

I phoned Sue several times during the following week. During one of these conversations, she told me that the "little white church on the corner," the one we had in mind for our wedding, just happened to be free for the date we had selected. She was bubbly and excited.

I hardly had the heart to caution her about asking too many people to the wedding or saying too much about it. After all, when you are in love, you want to tell everyone about it. And news gets around fast in a little community like Crestline.

The Navy instructors did not let up on us at school but kept drilling in medical facts, to make absolutely certain we knew what we would be doing, under any kind of pressure. I was glad I had made this choice of a career in the Navy, one that would be healing, not killing. I felt it was where He wanted me, and I knew I would be in a better position to spread the Word of God.

Some of the doctors who came in to lecture to us talked about healing processes, and how sometimes the power of God had taken over after they had done all they could medically and given up. One asked if there were any Christians in the group, and only a few of us raised our hands.

I think the doctor was trying to get through to us that there was another power in operation, guiding the physician, and speeding the recovery. I knew what he was driving at, but there were a lot of blank and skeptical faces. They wanted scientific facts for everything—nothing left up to some other force. It was frustrating to realize that while most of the guys acknowledged the increasing role of the unconscious mind in our lives, they failed to see how spiritual forces might be a factor in the healing process.

My head was full of medical stuff by the time I finished my schooling and we were ready to get married. We hadn't talked much about what we expected out of marriage, but we both knew we wanted to be together all the time. And in the beginning, we laid down one rule for both of us to follow. That rule was to tell each other what we were thinking, no matter how trivial, to discuss the least little thing that was bothering us before we went to sleep at night, and above all, to pray about it.

The day of our wedding arrived, and my friends did everything they could to see that all the details went smoothly. I had not seen Sue all day—just talked to her on the telephone—and, as far as I could tell, she was not having any of those nervous jitters and crying spells that you read about.

The minister of the church prayed with me before the service. I had told him just a brief history of myself when Sue and I talked with him on a previous visit, and he knew I was a bit uneasy about my "old friends" showing up or trying to ruin our service in some way. This prayer helped calm my nerves, and when we went out in the church to stand up front, I was delighted to see so many close friends.

As I waited for Sue to come down the aisle, I prayed—first, for her, then for myself. When the wedding march was played louder, and everyone stood up, my heart pounded, and tears came to my eyes, as I caught a glimpse of Sue on her father's arm. The radiant glow around her was breathtaking, and I saw several people reaching for their handkerchiefs, including my mother.

As we stood in front of the minister, I kept taking peeks at Sue and finally I caught her eye enough to wink at her and she smiled. I was not sure this was for real. I thought I was marrying an angel.

I know that God was with us that day. I could feel His presence. After the ceremony, we had a brief reception, and our parents and other relatives looked very happy. My mother had said that she hoped our marriage would last, and now at last, I think she was convinced it would!

Chapter Ten

We had to settle in San Diego quickly because I would have to report back to work at the Naval Training Center Dispensary. Sue did most of the moving in, which was not very hard since both of us came from small, furnished places. I had found a little apartment on Louisiana Street, near the Mission Valley area. It was hard for me to believe that I had a wife to come home to at the end of the day.

No one had bothered us during our wedding and we thought that, by now, the Brotherhood had given up. Sue was putting curtains up one evening during our first week in our new apartment when my scalp began to tingle, my hands began to shake, and my heart began thumping rapidly. From my experience in witchcraft, I knew what it was I felt. There were spirits present! Then I heard their voices—"If you want to follow this Jesus, then you'd better have the guts to go through what *He* did."

I sneered. "You crumbs can't panic me, man. *I've got Jesus.*"

The voices, like in a chorus, sneered right back. "Okay, so you got Jesus. Then you shouldn't mind following in His footsteps. Get down on the floor."

I tried to resist. I was glad they had chosen a time when Sue was present, so she could help pray for me.

Sue sensed what was happening, as I was pulled down on the floor. I was halfway down, when I felt myself being stretched out, my hands raised shoulder height and my feet springing together. I was in the position that Jesus had been on the cross.

I felt sharp pains in my hands and my feet and around my ankles and pain girding my head where Jesus had worn the crown of thorns. I experienced the sensation of blood coming from the palms of my hands. I fell on the floor as if someone had released me. Sue started praying, "Jesus, help us! Lift Satan from Mike's shoulders. Give us strength." She repeated the words over and over again until relief came.

I do not know what might have happened if I had not been a Christian. But after Sue had prayed for nearly an hour, I felt the grip of the demons leave me, and their weight lift from me. The pain eased and I got up, shaking my hands and rubbing at my ankles.

"We have to fight those demons and Satanists with prayer," Sue said. "We can't let down now." She hugged me around the waist and pressed her cheek against mine. I could feel her tears against my skin. "They must really want you back, but *I'm* not going to let them have you." When Sue got mad, you could see fire in her eyes, and I believed her.

We prayed during the day, and every night we asked God to help us. Soon we started going to Scott Memorial Baptist Church in San Diego, where we found a new friend in Pastor Tim LaHaye.

When he and his wife came to see us in our home, we told them about some of my past experiences with witchcraft, and about the oppression that still followed us. We were hoping he might have some answers for us, or some guidance that might help us oppose the Satanists.

"I've had some experiences along that line myself, Mike," Pastor LaHaye admitted. "I've been attacked by witches. Just what do you know of the overall picture, Mike? The total witchcraft scene?"

I shrugged. I had already told him I had been to an occult conference. "There were some weird guys that seemed to be the real backers of the whole thing," I said. "I heard the word *illuminati* . . ." I shook my head. "I never did find out much about them."

"That's because it's a top-secret organization, Mike. But I've done quite a bit of research. The Illuminati was started May 1, 1776, and the word itself means 'Holders of the Light.' In this case, it's a Satanic light. Members think they alone have the wisdom to run the world. It's really only the continuation of a Satanic organization that has been in existence since about 1100 A.D. Oh, under various names, of course."

Silence fell as we let Pastor LaHaye's words sink in. He continued, "We should be fighting it from a grass-roots level, educating people about how they can avoid falling into the traps of Satan, such as witchcraft and Satanism. You and Sue need a few more friends praying for you, that's the big thing—and you need to keep your faith strong. Our congregation is ready to help you, and we've got some very strong prayer warriors in our church."

Before Pastor LaHaye and his wife left, they prayed that the Lord would help us overcome this oppression. Knowing someone else would be praying for us really helped. But I still felt there were some loose ends dangling . . .

I had had the feeling for a long time that Sue and I had not learned *how* to pray effectively, that we lacked "prayer power," and that there were ways of prayer that could really defeat Satan in a big way—enough to put him down for the full count instead of having him get up off the canvas and come back at us with some new Satanic twist. I thought there must be a higher-powered prayer life than what we knew of yet.

Sue agreed with me. She was not one to give up on anything, but I could see she was beginning to have a few doubts about our ability to meet these demons or spirits head-on.

Just as we had settled into our apartment and were making new friends, we were transferred to Camp Pendleton, near Oceanside, about thirty-five miles north of San Diego.

"Do you have any idea how long we'll be here?" Sue asked me.

"Could be two years, from what I heard at work." Working with the Marines in medical supply, I did not dare bring up the subject of being shipped overseas. I had already learned that when you are in the service, it does not do much good to even think about things like that.

"Well, since we will be here for a while, would you mind too much if I got a job somewhere close by?"

I sighed. "I hate the thought of seeing you go to work, honey, but if it would give you more to do and bring in a little extra money to start a savings account with for the future . . . Gosh, what I earn as an E-3 does not go all that far."

"I was hoping you'd say that," she smiled. "I saw a sign in the Rexall Drug Store at Third and Hill. They need a fountain girl. I talked to the lady and she said she was hoping to get a Christian. But I wanted to ask you first."

"Go ahead and see what it would be like, if you want to." I was dubious about my Sue behind a counter as a soda jerk, but I knew a lot of the Navy wives had looked for jobs in the area, and jobs were scarce.

The next night Sue told me at the supper table that she had been hired by Mrs. Helen Hreha. "When I told her we were both Christians, she hired me on the spot, showed me around, and put me right to work. You'll have to meet her. She goes to the First Baptist Church and has invited us to come next Sunday."

We were so new in town that we decided to take Sue's employer up on her invitation to attend her church. We were delighted to learn that Mrs. Hreha was also the director of the Sunday School Primary Department.

Right after the church service, we were served coffee, and Helen made sure we were welcomed. Sue and I felt at home with this group, and we thanked the Lord for directing us to such a friendly church so quickly. Helen, Sue, and I clicked right away. Charles Lemmox was the pastor, and he was glad to hear that Sue and I might be interested in teaching a Sunday school class. But I was hesitant to accept.

"Let Sue and me pray about it," I told Helen. "I think you should know a little more about us before you have me teaching Sunday school. Why don't you drop by and see us sometime this week?"

On the way home, Sue seemed quiet. Then, just before we got in the door, she opened up. "Mike, why were you so enthusiastic about teaching Sunday school at first, then got all shook up about it?" She put her Bible on the table and sat down.

"Well, I just thought we ought to pray about it, first. I also think Helen should know about my witchcraft experiences and all that junk *before*—"

"How can you *say* that? You've accepted the Lord! Your sins are washed away. Jesus died for you. After all you've been through, you'd be a better teacher than a lot of goody-goodies that go around proclaiming how perfect they are!" Sue's eyes flashed, and I knew I had lost that argument already.

"Well," I drawled, "I think I ought to get stronger in the Lord!"

This stumped her for a minute, then she rallied. "I'll bet you'll have another adult helper, anyway. Are we going to give up now, when we've gotten this far in our Christian work? I thought this was one of the things you wanted to do?"

She had me there. She knew I liked working with kids of all ages, and she knew I needed a boost right now. I was getting restless about not being able to do more to witness for God. "Mike, there's something else."

"Oh, wow! How much *else?*" I laughed. "Boy, I wish you could see the sparks fly from your eyes—"

"Helen told me something of her life the other day, and she mentioned someone in her family had experience with witchcraft. So I'm sure she'll understand when you talk with her. She may even have some advice or help for us. I feel a great calm when I'm around her."

Helen came by that week, and we had a long discussion about how the Lord and Sue had helped me make a complete change of course in my life. When I finished, she remained silent for a while, and I held my breath. "Well, big-mouth Mike has done it again—blown it," I thought. "She'll probably fire Sue on the spot."

"Mike," she finally said, "I can understand why you might be hesitant to teach the young people. I can see you aren't afraid for yourself but only for the people you come in contact with. Don't worry, Mike. As head of the Sunday school—and I'm sure Pastor Lemmox will go along with me—I can tell you that we need young men like you, fellows who've been through something that gives them a conviction of witnessing for Christ. You can't fool those little kids today; they've learned too much from television. They can spot a phony right away. The class would be out of hand in no time!" She paused.

Sue smiled at me while Helen was talking, and I could see why Sue had dug her.

"Do you have any questions, Mike? We'll help you get started. You can have some lesson plans to study; then, when you're ready, I'll have someone to assist you. Maybe you have a friend out at the base you'd like to bring in. These young boys respond to you fellows in the Navy."

It ended up with Sue being assigned a class of second-grade girls, while I chose a class of third-grade boys.

In a couple of weeks, we felt ready to start teaching. As soon as I began talking with those kids, I realized I needed them more than they needed me. They were great from the start, and I was finding that the old smooth-talking orator was coming through in a different way now. These kids looked up to me, and not wanting to let them down or lead them astray, I strove desperately to make them realize how alive Jesus was—that He was a real person and could help them while they were growing up.

A short time later, we invited Mrs. Hreha over to discuss some of the lingering occult oppression we had been experiencing.

"Mike, Sue, I guess you two haven't heard of the power of the Blood, or you wouldn't be oppressed."

"Well," Sue said, cocking her head and trying to remember, "I think I read something about it quite a while ago."

"I've heard about it, but I never understood what it was all about," I added. "I never got around to checking it out."

"In Hebrews 9:11-14, it tells about Christ coming to put away the power of sin by dying for us," Mrs. Hreha explained. "Well, it's by the power of His shed Blood that He saved us, and when we claim this power, we claim the resurrection power of Jesus."

"How does that help in prayer?" I asked.

"When you pray, Mike, you have to remember that because Jesus shed His blood, you were saved. In Hebrews 9:22, it tells us that there is no remission of sin without the shedding of blood.

"In the Old Testament, people made blood sacrifices to God for their sins because they were under the law. Christ became for us the final sacrifice, and it was by His blood our sins were washed away, we were saved, and we became victorious over Satan, who *is*, right now, defeated."

"But how do you get this power, Helen?" Sue asked.

"Yeah, like, just what do you *say* to Christ?" I asked. "How can you humble yourself before Him and have the nerve to ask for power? That's what got me in trouble before: too much power."

Helen leaned back in her chair and laughed. "Mike, you challenge everything, don't you?"

"Yeah, and I once got into trouble for that, too."

Well, don't worry. I'm not leaving here until I'm sure you understand. You see, at salvation you invite this same power into your life. Once this is done, many Christians forget it is there and just coast along on the strength of that salvation-power experience," Helen explained.

"But why use it only once? You have the power in you; you can apply it to any and all occurrences in your life. If

157

the Blood can save you and wash away sins, it can surely take care of daily matters—even demon oppression.

"The Blood defeated death, which is Satan's greatest tool. He no longer holds the deed to our souls. By the power of the Blood, we were set free from death. Now we can call on this same power when Satan attacks our flesh, taking authority over him in the name of Jesus and reminding him of his defeat by the very Christ that lives in all who are born again!"

"It sounds so simple!" I said, almost laughing.

"Is there anything in particular that you say, Helen?" Sue asked.

"You have to get the idea of the Blood and Christ's suffering in your prayer, plus the specific need at the time. You could say, *Lord I ask for the power of Jesus to save me from this—name what the oppression is—and to help me with the problem I'm going through. I claim the protection of Jesus' Blood and the power of His resurrection to rebuke Satan, right now, in the name of Jesus!*"

I shook my head, hardly daring to believe that this would do it. "How about if I should come under oppression again or someone else should become oppressed?"

Helen laughed. "You just try it next time and tell me what happens. Once you have claimed this power, you won't be afraid to fight Satan."

"Thanks, Helen. I hope you know how much Mike and I appreciate this," Sue said. Helen prayed for us, asking God to strengthen our faith to fight Satan's encounters.

Not more than two days later, God permitted our faith and what Helen had said to be tested. We had not been asleep long that night when we both awoke and sat straight up in bed. A tall, black, humanlike figure was standing in the doorway of our bedroom. I started to get out of bed, saying, "What do you want?" Then I was suddenly lifted right out of bed and thrown onto the floor without having moved a muscle! Everything was black and dreamlike for a while.

"How did I get down here? Sue?" I pulled myself up and crawled onto the bed. The figure was gone.

"Mike, it worked! Are you all right?"

I put my arm around her and could feel her shaking. "What worked?"

"When the figure appeared, you were thrown onto the floor and started rolling around. I knew the demons were attacking you, so I claimed the power of the Blood over us and rebuked Satan like Helen said," Sue explained, "and he left!"

"Praise the Lord! Let's thank Him for being victorious!"

With this new confidence, Sue and I began to delve further into church work, and it also gave me a fresh outlook at work at the base. Even the man in charge of my detail, Tiny Clark, noticed a difference in my attitude toward other people. Tiny was a big guy, his 250 pounds well-distributed over his six-and-a-half-foot frame. He was always joking because the guys ribbed him about being so big, but I didn't think it really bothered him.

We had a break together one day, and over a cup of coffee, we got to know each other better. "I've heard you talking to guys about working for the Lord, Warnke. Do you really believe in all that?"

"Sure, I do, man. I've been through some rough scenes; and you'd better believe I probably wouldn't be here today if it wasn't for Him." I was reluctant to talk to my boss this way, but the thought came to me that he had to be interested or he would not have asked. "I was one of those smart-aleck hippies, Tiny," I said. "I came into the service because I didn't know what else to do, and two buddies of mine who were Christians began bugging me so much, I started listening, and what they said finally made sense. Since I started living for the Lord, my life has been changed."

"I used to be a Christian," Tiny said, rather sadly. "I just can't seem to get with it now, though." He got up and took our cups. "Well, I got to get back and see how these new guys are doing. Maybe we can talk again some time."

"Sure, Tiny. Anytime." I waved and made my way through the overcrowded mess hall. I didn't want to push him. I remembered only too well how Bob and Bill had almost turned me the other way a couple of times by coming on too strong.

Sue's Sunday school class was interesting to her and challenging, and she said the girls studied hard, but I began to have trouble in mine. I had started out being too easy on the boys, wanting them to think I was a nice guy, and before I knew it, they had taken over the class.

I tried to figure new ways to present the idea of Jesus to the boys, but I did not know how easily they misunderstood things and how stubborn and silly they could be, all within one hour on a Sunday morning. I finally talked to Helen about it.

"Why don't you see if you can find someone to help you, Mike. I've exhausted my list, trying to find some more teachers. Isn't there anyone out at the base who would like to help out? I know boys that age can get pretty tiring and hard to handle." Helen hurried off to see about another class.

I stood there wondering how I had ever gotten into this. With no real hope of finding anyone, I nonetheless started running through the names of guys I worked with who might be able to help. "Hmmm!" I suddenly beamed. "Tiny! Why hadn't I thought of him before? Maybe this would be the perfect way of bringing him back—he said he was a Christian—once."

The next morning, I approached Tiny and asked him to join me for a cup of coffee again. We had been talking more lately, but so far I had not mentioned anything about needing help at Sunday school.

When we got seated, I came right out with it: "You know, the other day I told you about teaching those third-grade boys in Sunday school? Well, I didn't tell you the whole story. I was so anxious to make a good impression on these boys and to be their friend that I was too nice, a people-pleaser. Now, they're running over me, and I can't handle them."

Tiny looked at me in surprise. "I thought you had all the confidence in the world, Mike. What happened?"

I looked around the crowded room. Guys were coming and going, and no one was sitting too close to us. "Tiny, if you've got some time, I'll tell you what really happened to me." This would be the first time I had told anyone other than those from whom I was receiving spiritual guidance anything about my witchcraft experiences. Still, I hesitated.

"You're lucky, Mike," Tiny said. "I'm too much of a sinner to be acceptable to the Lord. You don't know what I've done. And I drink, Mike. Do you know that? I have to have my bottle to get to sleep. I'm just plain no good, and Jesus wouldn't have me on a bet."

"Bet *me!*" I exploded. Anyone who tried to compete with Mike Warnke when it came to being *bad* had a fight on his hands. So I gave it to him, full blast. I did not smooth over anything. I also told him about the oppression Sue and I had been under, and how Helen had come over one night and told us about the power of the Blood.

"Having a big guy like you in class to help with the kids would really ease my mind, Tiny. How about it?" I waited for an answer. Then I looked at him. He was burying his face in his hands. "Hey, what's with you?"

"I'm such a big slob," he spluttered. "Feeling sorry for myself, and thinking I was so rotten. Man, I've been a Boy Scout compared to you."

I shrugged. "It's no big thing; He died for our sins, remember? He *will* forgive you."

"Well, if you could do it—give yourself to Jesus—I can. I want to do it right now, Mike. I want to give my heart to Christ."

"Good." I waited while Tiny prayed silently. "Okay? Now, then, how about putting your faith into action. How about my proposition?"

"What's that?"

"Helping me in Sunday school?"

"Sunday school?"

I went into the whole thing again.

"I'll give it a try." He sighed.

"Uh, Tiny, I'd appreciate you not saying anything to anyone around here about this witchcraft business."

"Yeah. I know what you mean," Tiny answered. "Well, I'll see you on Sunday."

I sat there for another few minutes, thinking about what I had told Tiny. It had kind of shaken me up as well as him, pouring it all out again, but I had noticed a difference in the way he had responded. "Maybe it doesn't hurt to tell it like this, now, as long as I use it to witness for the Lord," I thought. I could hardly wait to tell Sue I had found some help, and how Tiny, after hearing my story, had recommitted himself to the Lord.

When I introduced my new assistant to the boys the next Sunday, there were many giggles. "Fellows, this is 'Tiny' Clark, and he's going to be helping me out. If any of you wonder how strong he is, just ask him. In the meantime, maybe we can get back to work in this class."

From that Sunday on, there was not a peep out of those boys. They kept getting his name mixed up and called him "Teensy" instead of Tiny, and soon he became "Teensy Tiny." They were so awed by his size, and he was so good-natured to them, they never caused any more trouble, and it all helped me become a better teacher. I could tell Tiny enjoyed this work, and it was fun to watch him growing in the Lord.

Sue and I got so busy with our church work, our jobs, and some of the extra committees that we were both on, that before I knew it, we had been at the First Baptist Church for almost two years. I had been appointed the assistant deacon of the primary church, and whenever I had a chance, I talked to the high-school group. Those kids were really great, but I noticed a few of them were beginning to stray from the church, just as I had at that age.

One night, I was led to tell them about my experiences in witchcraft, and the response after the meeting was something to behold! Many of the kids came up to me afterward and wanted to know more.

After I got home that night and woke Sue up to tell her

about my experience with the high-schoolers, she got quite excited. "Maybe you should start telling about your witch-craft experiences more often in your testimony." She yawned. "I'm sorry I didn't stay awake until you came in, honey. I don't know what's the matter with me lately. I keep getting so sleepy—even at work, right after lunch."

"Maybe you'd better quit or see a doctor. You may be getting run down or need vitamins or something."

I had a hard time sleeping that night. I was keyed up after the meeting with the young people. I could still see their faces as they listened eagerly to what I was saying.

It was still on my mind, when I woke up the next morning. I was thinking Tiny could take over my class, and they could find someone to help him, I thought. Those teenagers were facing even more problems today than I had been at their age, and if someone had only warned me . . .

Before I could ask Tiny about taking my class or talk to Helen about working with the young people, one of my officers handed me a bombshell: *shipping orders!*

They wanted me in Vietnam—like, now. They hardly gave me enough time to pack my seabag.

Sue took it better than I did. It was not until the day I said good-bye to her at the terminal that she broke down and cried. "Remember, how I kept complaining about getting sleepy? Well, I'm pretty sure that I—we—"

"Praise the Lord! You mean—?"

She nodded.

I wanted to laugh and cry at the same time.

"I'll stay at Mother's, in Crestline. I—I hope you get back before he's born," she sobbed.

"She," I corrected, fighting back tears myself.

Chapter Eleven

In the back of my mind for a long time had been the almost-certain knowledge that I would be going to Vietnam sooner or later. But I guess I was still not past the point of playing let's-pretend games with myself. There was so much to do in re-making my personality, and there had been so little time. My newfound Christianity had a long way to go yet, to seep into all the recesses of my soul. Oh, Sue and I *thought* that accepting Christ, witnessing for Him was all we had to do. Learning about the power of the Blood, now, that was really progress! Yet, Jesus' love had still not taught me to stop playing games with myself.

It seemed such a short time since I had met Sue—and Jesus. Now I would be separated from Sue for a long time. What if something should happen to me? I guess I felt I would be leaving Jesus behind, too. With Sue beside me, I had successfully counteracted the oppression of the Satanists and fought them down. But as I was about to find out, I had not completely won the battle going on in my own soul, after all.

When we landed in Nam, I was thrust into a streaming, bloody inferno.

There was no time to think, things happened so fast. Satan worshiping was hell; Vietnam was also hell, on an unbelievable scale. Seeing the horrible massacre around me as the hot rain beat down incessantly, I could not believe Christ was within a thousand miles, and I was convinced I had left Jesus behind—or that He had left me.

In this world I was seeing, everything was against you: the oppressive heat, against which there is no defense and which presses down on you like a huge, hot hand; the mosquitoes that not only provoke you into unceasing swatting when you do not really have the energy to even raise your hand but which also transmit diseases that can tear you apart as bad as the bombs; the fighting and the constant, absolute ignorance of who is friendly and who is not; the mud that gets into everything and pulls at your every step when you try to move; and the very water you drink, full of dysenteric bacteria. I thought I had left pills behind, but in Vietnam you have to swallow several pills every day just to stay alive, to fight the malaria, and to overcome the effects of the heat. You even have to put pills into your drinking water.

I tried to live my Christian testimony at first, but the immediate frustrations of the war took my eyes off the Lord, hampering my Bible reading, my witnessing and prayer life—everything. My faith was weakening fast!

The pills keep your body functioning. To keep your mind from going off the deep end, you *drink*. It was very difficult to find Jesus Christ in the jungles, but alcohol was plentiful. It was almost too easy for anyone who had been off the bottle to get back on and quick. There was a daily beer ration, and in the various clubs, getting liquor was no problem, either.

My first imbibing was part of the game I was still playing. I would tell myself I was sick. I had a headache. My stomach was upset. It was easy to find some excuse to take a snort. And then another.

I had chosen to go to Hospital Corps School because I thought being a medic was really right-on in Christ, saving lives and comforting the wounded. I remember reading about Walt Whitman, male nurse of the Civil War and the first free-swinging poet who could see good in almost anything. And on paper the duties of a Navy corpsman in Vietnam were high-sounding: "To give aid and comfort to wounded Marines." But out in the field, it didn't quite work that way . . .

When a Marine up in the front lines is hit, it is up to the corpsman to get to him, no matter what is going on, whether they are flinging all the scrap metal from hell at you, waiting in trees to drop charge-loaded coconuts on your head, or hiding in the brush to watch you walk into one of their clever little booby traps.

You pack up your "dollies and dishes" and beat feet across this field or that monster-infested roaring torrent, and you jump over this hill or crash through that thorny tangle of vines—Check! That's all in the game, and you knew the dangers you were up against—No sweat. You agreed to put your life on the line to help your men.

But what happens next? When you get to your fallen comrade, there are very likely a lot of Viet Cong already there, attending to him—stripping his body, torturing him, preparing to slaughter him, rehearsing his funeral. I had thought saving lives was really praising the Lord. They had not told me that to save one life, I might very well have to take others.

They knew it, though. Some say corpsmen are not supposed to carry weapons, but I was issued a .45 when I got to Vietnam, and I was allowed to carry any weapon I wanted the whole time I was there. I had an M-16, grenades, and even a shotgun at various times. I was stationed in I-Corps Area, north of Da Nang, three miles from the De-Militarized Zone, operating out of Vandergrift Combat Base.

When you had secured your patient, then you ascertained the nature and extent of his injuries. If he had a simple bullet hole, you cleaned the wound and put on battle dressing—a big gauze pad. Then you wired a chit to the wounded man's clothing and called a Medevac chopper. The chit gave the details, name of man, diagnosis, etc.

If he had lost much blood, you would set up a transfusion bottle for him. If he was in shock, you treated him for shock, keeping him warm and his feet elevated. If he was mangled, and many were—well, you just did all you could to stop the bleeding and save what was left.

The treating of the wounded did not get to me, since I was trained in this and knew what to expect. What did get to me afterward was the irony of having to kill people in order to save the lives of the wounded. Too many times we had to fight our way *to* a wounded Marine who was crying out for help. There was no time to sit down and have a debate about ethics then. All I knew was that VC or NVR's who could see my Red Cross armband and helmet were trying to kill me to keep me from my patient.

I was in charge of three platoons, and we cared for about one hundred twenty-five men. I was with the command platoon. As a reinforced company, we had two mortar squads, two machine-gun squads, two forward artillery observers, a forward aircraft observer, and a couple of M-79 grenade-launchers.

By this time, I had started drinking for non-medicinal purposes. Several things accounted for this: One of the two times I cried while I was overseas, was shortly after I arrived, when a buddy of mine was killed—a mortar shell landed directly on him, disintegrating him except for his shoes. This incident, along with the general carnage and bloodshed, was getting to my head, and liquor was readily available to me, especially after I had been there for a while and made a lot of friends, one of them being in charge of stocking the officers' club. It was easy for me to get it, because I bought it from employees through the back door. Then, too, I often received gifts of whiskey from a guy whose life I had pulled out of the fire.

I was never busted for anything, because I was able to talk my way out of any scrape I was in, and, as far as drinking is concerned, I was able to maintain my cool while drunk, unless I got so drunk that I passed out, in which case, they do not bother you anyway.

It got to the point where I was existing from one bottle to the next, and the whole rotten jungle was bathed in an alcoholic fog, in the shadows of which lurked the most diabolical dragons you could imagine. As always, when Mike Warnke did something, including backsliding, he did it in a big way.

One incident which made me clutch the bottle even tighter happened when one of the natives wandering around in our area was discovered to be a spy, and the message he was carrying was a detailed description of myself and the skipper, identifying us as prime targets for the Viet Cong. His "trial," if you can call it that, amounted to an officer pronouncing the mandatory death sentence on the spot. The spy was to be summarily shot. The officer cast about for an appropriate executioner, and seeing no one else, settled on me. "You'll do, Warnke."

"Do what, sir?"

"Execute him."

Some guys were tying him to a tree.

"Shoot him?"

"What else?"

I went faint. At that point in my sojourn in Vietnam, I had prided myself on having thus far escaped a rescue situation where I would have to kill someone. Now I had to kill a guy who was not blasting away at me or about to administer the *coup de grace* to a fallen Marine, a guy who could not even run.

"Well," the officer barked, "get it over with!"

Time did not stand still. There was no time. No time to think, let alone pray, and it had been a long time since I had done any of that. What I did was the worst thing I have ever done in my life. I did what I was told. I got it over with. I shot a spy, went to my tent, cooked dinner, and ate. And something died inside of me.

The second incident happened after we had been in the bush for forty-five days straight without a break, when we were abruptly recalled to the rear, to "stand lines." By stateside standards, it was no picnic, but compared with "out there," where we lived in deep mud, slept in lean-tos, dodged bugs and bullets, and ate cold food sprinkled with dirt and bugs, it was great.

After three weeks of standing the lines away from active bush duty, we were hysterical with delight to learn that we were now about to be given an additional in-country "R and R"—rest and relaxation. When we were landed at our destination, we could not believe it. Our whole company crawled out of the transport boat to greet —the *beach!* We were at Qua Viet, on the ocean, for four days of steaks, beer, ocean air, sunning, and lazing around. We were in heaven.

Oh, so sorry . . . forget the beach and the sun; we were overtaken by a raging typhoon. No matter, we still could rest and have a good time in our tents, drinking, playing cards, making our own fun, while we grinned at the impo-tent forces outside, incapable of dampening our spirits, after the fiery and bloody hell we had been through.

Most of us were in a good mood.

But for a few, the sudden idleness gave ground to dark-ness. There were racial disturbances. And worse, under the circumstances, there was an undercurrent of deep-rooted dislike of the new Skipper and some of his mates. In Vietnam, if you are an officer and you are unpopular with your men, you stand a good chance of having "an accident." They call it "fragging."

I was sitting on my cot one night as the windblown rain lashed against the tent walls, when, through all that noise, I heard a terrific explosion, and immediately a call ringing out for a corpsman—on the double!

I grabbed my bag and flashlight and ran out into the storm. The tents were like floating islands, and I was in water up to my ankles. The wind jerked me around like it had hands. I grabbed the first Marine I saw, yelling, "C'mon," and took the lead to the source of the explosion.

I was the first to enter the tent, its sides ripped to shreds. I shone my flashlight in there and saw a radio oper-ator I knew, a Hawaiian. He was floating face-up in the ankle-deep water red with blood. A large hole gaped over his right eye.

Others were moaning and screaming. A black kid's legs were all lumpy and bloody, and another guy had a jagged piece of shrapnel in his chest.

As we reconstructed it later, these guys had been huddled around a field stove to keep warm and dry out some of their blankets. The assassins—our own guys—who had mistaken the radio operators' tent for the officers', had raced by outside in the blinding rain, whipped open the tent flap, and tossed in a fragmentation grenade. The grenade had landed squarely in their midst.

Eight of the occupants were critically injured; two died. Some of them had multiple shrapnel wounds in the face.

That finished off whatever sense of moral outrage might have remained in me.

Sue wrote to me almost every day, but the mail situation being affected by battle conditions and shot-down helicopters, I might go for two or three weeks without getting any mail at all. During this time, I had to brace myself against the bitter disappointment of not hearing from her and from others for whom I cared. Sometimes these eternities of silence happened just when things were really rough.

Then, suddenly, I would receive a whole deulge of mail. At such times, I would have to fortify myself against a complete emotional crack-up. I tried hard not to think about what Sue would think if she knew how far from the Lord I had slid. The thought haunted me.

On top of everything else, or perhaps because of it, I had constructed a shield of armor plate around me that would not allow a single emotion to enter or leave. I could no longer react to anything; my voltage-input regulators had long since been overloaded and burned out. I didn't realize it then, but without the reality of Jesus, this is the mind's only defense mechanism, to keep from going off the deep end.

Surgeons go through years of pre-med, med school, internship, and so on, during which time they learn the knack of temporarily suspending their emotions to some degree, and yet they do not become bloodless zombies. But for me, just barely saved from one dimension of hell, and so soon ordered to kill in cold blood and then having to kill to keep others from dying, and being constantly exposed to the horribly, painfully mutilated, it was too much.

But I am not going to take myself off the hook. In self-pity, in resentment, in just plain weakness, I gave up. Had I clung tenaciously to Jesus. I know now that I could have come through it, His way. But even now, I thank God for allowing it all to happen, for showing me how desperately I need Him—always.

I had lost my faith, but praise God, Sue had not lost hers. Her prayers were in large measure responsible for my coming home alive at all. There were simply too many close calls, too many flesh wounds that should have been fatal. Even in the depths of my mindless despondency, the Lord was protecting me.

I was often loaded when I received mail from Sue. I only answered about half of her letters. Still, she kept writing, never giving up—knowing from the things I wrote and the tone of my letters that I was a mess. She would quote Scriptures even though I made no effort to reciprocate.

One passage was from I John 1:4-7: *And these things write we unto you, that your joy may be full. This then is the message which we have heard of him, and declare unto you, that God is light, and in him is no darkness at all. If we say that we have fellowship with him, and walk in darkness, we lie, and do not the truth: But if we walk in the light, as he is in the light, we have fellowship one with another, and the blood of Jesus Christ his Son cleanseth us from all sin.*

I felt the emotion *almost* piercing through my armor that time. I had once wanted to be a source of His light myself.

In another letter, Sue wrote that she knew I was exposed to death almost constantly, and she wished she could be at my side. "I pray for your safety and good spirits," she went on, "even though I can't be there to comfort you, but I know He is trying to get near you for me. I have the awful feeling that you have closed up like a shell. He can help you face death, Mike, because He had to face it."

By this time, it didn't register. Nothing registered. I had lost all response to death . . . or anything else.

But all things on this earth must eventually come to an end, and in October of 1969, my unit was finally withdrawn from Vietnam and sent to Okinawa as part of President Nixon's troop withdrawal plan.

I was really flipped by this time. One guy thought I was schizophrenic. "You're like a stone, Warnke," one of the medical officers said. "We can't even make you mad anymore. I think you had better see the psychiatrist. You're in no shape to be sent back to the States. They'll think we don't treat our boys right in the Navy." He looked at me intently, to see if he might have finally gotten to me.

I just shrugged. "What time do I go?"

Alone with the head doc, I sat in the comfortable leather lounge chair he offered. After a few preliminary pleasantries, he got down to it. "Most of my patients express surprise that I don't ask them to lie on a couch and tell me the first thing that comes to their minds when I say a word, for example, 'cat' . . ."

"Mouse," I interrupted.

"Hmmm," he murmured, tapping his pencil.

During the sessions I had with him, Dr. McPherson tried all the tricks of his trade, and eventually, I'm afraid that my stubbornness caused him to abandon a couple of pet psycho-innovations he thought were destined to revolutionize psychiatry. He tried free association, dream interpretation, ink blots, non-directive psychology, group counseling, and structured interviewing. He tried to get me to play roles, and he even threatened to put me on drugs and shock therapy.

Finally, after a long tense interview one humid afternoon, *he* broke down and cried. At least, he had tears in the corners of his eyes.

"Believe me, Mike, I'm really unhappy for *your* sake that I couldn't get you to loosen up emotionally. It'll tear you apart sooner or later, keeping it all in like this. Especially a man like you, who is basically an emotional guy. People have died of heart attacks because of the constriction of muscles in the throat and chest area—a physical manifestation of the mental noose you have made for yourself. Try to laugh. Or cry. Or *something*. From what you have told me of your religious experience, the only real hope I can see for you is to—get right with God!"

That came the nearest of anything he had said or done to pierce my shell.

Then, after man had done all he could do, God stepped in. A short while later, I got some news from the Red Cross that made me actually break loose and cry—the second time I cried while overseas. It was a message from Sue, informing me that I was the father of an eight-pound son—Brendon Michael Warnke.

I sobbed out my thanks to God. For my son, and for His. And I started on the long road back.

Chapter Twelve

We were making our final approach to El Toro Marine Air Station in Orange County, California, on March 1, 1970. It had been a long flight, with more than half a dozen departure delays from Okinawa and another delay in San Francisco, making our arrival in El Toro at night.

Just as the wheels of the jet chirped on the landing strip, I got all soft and shaky like jelly with the anticipation of seeing Sue again and my three-month-old son for the first time. I was worrying about how much of my backsliding would be evident on my face and in my conversation, but I had gotten back to God and knew He was already working deep inside to straighten me out.

As I stepped off the plane and saw Sue in the crowd, I felt a sense of overpowering relief—I was home! I rushed down the passageway to her and grabbed her in my arms.

"Oh, Sue!" was all I could say.

"Welcome home, Mike," she managed, breaking off in a sob.

And we hugged each other so hard, we could scarcely breathe.

After a while, Sue pulled back and said, "You've lost weight, honey. Didn't they feed you over there?"

"I lost quite a lot of things over there," I murmured.

And, wow! Brendon Michael turned out to be really something! He had my nose and eyebrows and Sue's sweet smile, at least when Sue was feeding him.

"I've shown him your photograph every day and explained to him that you were his daddy, so don't be surprised if that's the first word he comes out with."

I laughed. He certainly was a bouncer, and I was determined that he would have a better upbringing than the son of Al "Whitey" Warnke.

It did not take long to get settled in San Diego.

We had two weeks to rest and become a family again in our cozy little apartment before I had to report back to duty at Balboa Naval Hospital. I had re-enlisted in the Navy for six more years in order to receive a bonus and to get specialized medical training in the cardio-pulmonary school.

As the days blended into weeks, it became clear that Sue pretty well guessed what had happened in Vietnam. In line with our practice of telling each other everything, I gradually revealed what she had sensed, but instead of being disappointed in me, she blamed herself for not praying harder.

The cardio-pulmonary school taught me how to help doctors diagnose and treat diseases of the heart and lungs. I learned how to operate complex computerized equipment with such names as the Godard Pulmonary Tester, Collins Spirometer, IL Blood Gas Analyzer, Sanborn Cardiac Monitors, Cordis Dye Injector, Scholander Gas Analyzer, and the Van Slyke Gas Analyzer.

Despite the fact that I wanted Christ first in my life again, despite all that He had brought me through and saved me from, despite all the lessons I had learned, I put up a stiff resistance. Although Sue and I started back to church regularly on my return, I sensed that I was not operating with Christ first. Perhaps the particular services we attended were not dynamic enough for my needs at this time. Also, I felt that even though Sue and I had learned how to claim the Blood, and this helped us in many ways, there was still another dimension of Christianity that we were not getting.

One evening after I had come home from the service school, I answered a knock on the door. There was a couple on the doorstep. The man said rather loudly, "Praaaise God! Does Jeeesus live here?"

I recognized the woman as someone we had met at church in Oceanside—Janelle. I was startled but said, "Yes, come in and find out."

Janelle said, "Mike, I'd like you to meet my evangelist husband, Dick Handley. The Lord told us you were having a rough faith walk, and we came to see if there is anything we can do." She looked around. "Where's Sue?"

"In the nursery, feeding the baby," I said. "I'll get her."

But Sue had heard our voices and came out, just as I turned around. "He's asleep. Praise the Lord, it's the Handleys!"

Sue showed them around our apartment and let them peek in at the baby. Dick noticed on the wall a painting that we had bought in Tijuana. It was of a man with a wild-eyed appearance. "That's a horrible picture," he said. "He looks Satanic to me."

"*Horrible?* Terrific work of art, you mean. Look at the use of color, the lifelike tones, and the way the guy used his brush."

Dick shuddered. He shook his head. "You ought to take it down."

"Hah! It cost me a bundle, but I'll think about it."

"Well, anyway, Mike. The important thing is, we know you've been having problems, and we think we have the answer for you."

"What is it?"

"Have you ever heard of the Baptism in the Holy Spirit."

"The *what?*"

"The Baptism in the Holy Spirit."

"Don't give me that 'Baptism in the Holy Spirit' stuff," I said, sitting down and clenching my hands together. "Sue and I believe in the Bible and in being saved, and we pray all the time. We *know* who Jesus is, and we've both been baptized, so—"

"I know you took Jesus into your heart, but until you're baptized in the Holy Spirit—"

"I accepted Jesus when I was in boot camp—in a mop closet. My only problem now is to live up to being a Christian. I know the Lord is helping me. I don't need to be a Holy Roller or whatever." Dick chuckled at my remark. "All I have to do is study the Scriptures more and re-learn how to feel and then how to control my emotions."

I *had* started letting loose lately, but learning how to handle my emotions was something else again. Right now, I kept thinking about how pushy Dick Handley had been, coming into my apartment and criticizing my art work. Maybe he preferred abstract art.

"Mike, I didn't intend to tell you to do anything. You can't get it by doing things."

"Get what?"

"The Holy Spirit. When we receive the gift of God's Holy Spirit, we enter a new dimension of discipleship to our Blessed Lord."

"But why do I need this Baptism?" I questioned him as Sue listened intently for his answer.

"Immediately when we receive the infilling of the Holy Spirit, He begins some housecleaning in our lives. Things which used to bother us no longer do so. Fears, irritations, and resentments begin to fall away. We begin to see people differently—more as God sees them. The Spirit will also show us some more obstinate wrongs in our lives—some sins we hardly realized were there. And by the supernatural empowering of the Spirit, we are given the desire and the will to stand against them."

Janelle smiled. "Look what happened to the disciples in Acts, chapter two, when they received the Baptism in the Holy Spirit: they couldn't *help* but go out and spread the Word. They had a new power from God which stayed with them and just took over, like, well—"

"Like an automatic pilot, Mike," Dick said.

I shook my head. "That's getting too far out for me. I think God gives you a brain to use. He gives it to you, and it is up to you to take it from there. I accepted Christ, I

177

went through water baptism at Scott Memorial, and now it's *my* responsibility."

"It's *not*. It's Jesus' . . . if you'll just let Him take over. Yield to His will, Mike and Sue. Ask Him for this power, and He will be your guidance system."

But I could not see it their way. I thought they were weird fanatics. "He's nuts," I told Sue later. I figured it was up to me to generate my own power. Why should I expect Jesus to lay it all on a silver platter for me?

Feeling this way about it, for the next few weeks after their visit, I tried especially hard to increase my own horsepower. I made vows and resolutions. I set the alarm and forced myself to read the Bible at certain times every day. Naturally, Sue helped me in this. A good time for me to read the Bible aloud was when Sue was feeding Brendon his early morning bottle at 5:30 A.M. At the hospital I read as much as I could during break times and made a regular practice of reading right after dinner. I read aloud while Sue did the dishes, then had her read aloud while I got my uniform and shoes in shape for the next day.

The schedule I had set up for myself was getting to me, wearing me down. I spent quite a lot of time on my knees in prayer, but instead of feeling uplifted, I was feeling beaten down. It was helping me to feel emotion, all right, but it was the wrong emotion—like, anger, man. I was getting mad.

We had been very friendly with Tom and Diane Speakman, parents of six children, who lived in Crestline. Sue met them while I was overseas. She frequently attended a Bible study held at their home. They came down to San Diego several times to visit with us and have prayer meetings, and we went up to Crestline to return these visits.

Tom was definitely thinking of moving to San Diego, where job prospects were better. On one of their weekend visits to our apartment, Sue and I could tell Diane had something she could hardly wait to tell us. They had left their children with a relative for the weekend, so we were relaxed, our baby being asleep and not due to wake up the whole night, hopefully.

"Some of us in the Bible study group have had a new experience, and it's out of this world," Diane finally blurted out.

"That's for sure." Tom grinned.

"You'll never guess what happened to me," Diane continued, looking at us.

"You found out you're going to have another baby," Sue said.

Diane laughed. "In a way, I guess. We got the Baptism in the Holy Spirit."

"Oh Lord," I exclaimed. "Here we go again. You, too, Tom?"

"Yes, praise God! We didn't know it, but it's what we have been seeking for all this time."

"What Mike means is, he doesn't dig the Baptism in the Holy Spirit," Sue explained.

"Well, uh," I didn't want to hurt their feelings, "I just think when you ask Jesus to enter your heart, He comes in, and that's it. You have to do your own growing after that. Read the Bible to see it like it is, and do what it says. What more is there?"

I had asked for it. I found out what more there is. They talked about Dave Wilkerson and his success in getting tough kids, like myself, into Jesus' camp, and not only that, but helping a number of them eventually to get the Baptism. "He didn't have it easy, Mike," Tom pointed out. "Wilkerson fought an uphill battle."

"But he got some of the roughest New York hoodlums to get on their knees," Diane elaborated. "One of the worst of them was Nicky Cruz. There's a book out by him, now. He gave up his gang and accepted Christ, and after months and months of struggling and learning, just about the time he was ready to give up and run away, he suddenly received the Holy Spirit."

We had the books by Wilkerson and Cruz in our apartment, and we knew what Diane was talking about—it was all right for them.

"Did you read what Acts 1:5-11 says about the Baptism?" Diane opened her Bible and read, *"For John truly baptized with water; but ye shall be baptized with the Holy Ghost not many days hence. When they therefore were come together, they asked of him, saying, Lord, wilt thou at this time restore again the kingdom to Israel? And he said unto them, It is not for you to know the times or the seasons, which the Father hath put in his own power. But ye shall receive power, after that the Holy Ghost is come upon you: and ye shall be witnesses unto me both in Jerusalem, and in all Judaea, and in Samaria, and unto the uttermost part of the earth. And when he had spoken these things, while they beheld, he was taken up; and a cloud received him out of their sight. And while they looked stedfastly toward heaven as he went up, behold, two men stood by them in white apparel; Which also said, Ye men of Galilee, why stand ye gazing up into heaven? this same Jesus, which is taken up from you into heaven, shall so come in like manner as ye have seen him go into heaven."*

"Later," Diane said, "after a lot of discussion among the apostles, the Bible says in Acts 2:1-4: *And when the day of Pentecost was fully come, they were all with one accord in one place. And suddenly there came a sound from heaven as of a rushing mighty wind, and it filled all the house where they were sitting. And there appeared unto them cloven tongues like as of fire, and it sat upon each of them. And they were all filled with the Holy Ghost, and began to speak with other tongues, as the Spirit gave them utterance."*

"Now, wait a minute," I said. "I read that before, too, but it's symbolic! It's a symbolic baptism, like using water, only you aren't. What's that got to do with power, or anything? I was baptized in water, and it was more real than what you're talking about because they used *something*— water." I spread my hands. "If something tangible like water won't cleanse my sins away for good, how can just *thinking* we're being baptized do it?"

We spent hours talking and studying and reading and rereading. We pulled out some of the books, like Wilkerson's *The Cross and the Switchblade*, Cruz's *Run Baby Run*, Frost's *Aglow with the Spirit* and Sherrill's *They Speak in Other Tongues* and a lot of Scriptures.

Diane pointed out, "In John 1:32-34, it says, *And John bare record, saying, I saw the Spirit descending from heaven like a dove, and it abode upon him. And I knew him not: but he that sent me to baptize with water, the same said unto me, Upon whom thou shalt see the Spirit descending, and remaining on him, the same is he which baptizeth with the Holy Ghost. And I saw, and bare record that this is the Son of God.*

"See?" Diane continued. "There's another distinction between baptizing with water and baptizing with the Holy Spirit. John could baptize with water, but only Jesus can baptize in the Holy Ghost." She beamed triumphantly as though she had shattered my final argument, but I was too stubborn for it.

In fact, I exploded. Sweeping my hands toward the various books scattered on the coffee table, end tables, and floor, I yelled, "Okay, okay! I don't know these people—Wilkerson, Cruz, the others. So I don't trust them."

"You know us, Mike," Diane pointed out in a soft voice.

"Yeah, I know you. But you're getting pretty emotional about this whole thing; you're getting carried away, and I don't know if I can trust you, either!"

"If you'd just have an open mind about it, Mike," Tom pleaded.

"I know one thing," I said. "I trust Jesus, and if Jesus wants to give me this, if this is something He wants me to have, He'll give it to me. I'll ask Him, and if He gives it to me, then I'll know it is something He wants me to have."

"It still won't work, if you don't have an open mind and heart," Tom repeated.

"Mike, *you're* the one who's emotional about it," Diane said. "But I guess that's good, in your case. When you feel a touch of God's presence, it is bound to affect your emotions. Love is an emotion, and that is God's manifestation of love to us!"

"All right, there's no time like the present to try," I said, getting down on my knees, resting my elbows on the sofa, and burying my face in my hands. I was actually crying. I was utterly beaten down by the words, the truth, and by my own frustrations—my bloody memories of war and my stabbing guilt about killing.

It was all swelling through me now, and I suddenly felt I *did* need something more than my own power, after all, to get going. Of course, I did not want to admit it to them. The worst thing was, I was mortally afraid that I would go through all this and prove them right.

"Dear Lord," I prayed aloud. "If it is Your will for me to be blessed with the Baptism in the Holy Spirit, let me have it, Lord. Give me all of it!"

Tom had his hands on my shoulders, and Sue and Diane were on their knees on both sides of me. I could hear Sue weeping, and it gave me a pang to think how the girl I loved so deeply had gone through such agony for me and with me.

"Give Mike the Holy Spirit, Jesus," Sue said, managing to keep her voice from splintering too much.

"O Christ, be with Mike, now," Diane said. "Give him what You gave me, Jesus, precious Savior. He needs You, Lord. He needs the power of the Holy Spirit more than any of us."

"We claim Your promise, Jesus. Send the fullness of Your Spirit to him right now," Tom added.

Sue and Diane were both crying now. "Praise You, Jesus!" Diane said. "Give Mike the chance. Let him be ready to receive Your strength. Oh, Jesus—" and she broke off into a language I didn't recognize, but the power of those words cut into my innermost being and ignited a fire.

"Hallelujah!" Tom said. "Praise the Lord."

An overwhelming sense of power and peace filled the room. Everyone was praising God.

I was shaking. I seemed to be riding on a tide of love and wonder. I began to feel weightless, giddy. Colors whirled around. My heart was pounding rapidly and my breath sucking in large gulps as I began to feel the muscles in the back of my neck twitch and my skin prickle.

A gold white brilliance shone inside my closed eyelids, and I felt something like cool fire filling my lungs and from there, radiating to all the cells of my body, making me tinglingly alive. And then a strange language came forth from my own mouth.

It seemed as though the doors and windows of our apartment had suddenly been thrown open, because the air which brushed my skin was so fresh and pure. I felt a cleansing within my heart, and I was lifted to a new sense of God's power and love. At last, I experienced His peace. "Thank You, Jesus!"

Chapter Thirteen

"I love you, honey!" I grabbed Sue around the waist and hugged her the next morning. "I forget whether I told you I loved you or not last night. I was so excited about receiving the Baptism in the Holy Spirit. But—gee, I wish you could have, too . . ."

"But I did, Mike," she said, squeezing me.

"Oh, you're putting me on, baby. You didn't say anything . . ."

"It was your show, Mike. Anyway, one at a time." She giggled. "But I received right beside you. And I spoke in an unknown language, too."

"Praise the Lord! I never even heard you."

"How could you, when you were being so blessed?"

I danced her around the kitchen, and we whooped and sang, "Amazing grace! How sweet the sound, that saved a wretch like me! I once was lost but now am found, was blind but now I see . . ."

Late that afternoon, we said good-bye to the Speakmans. Relaxing in the living room, I said, "So, we've got the Holy Spirit. So now what?"

We found out "now what" during the next few weeks. We discovered that when you have the Baptism in the Holy Spirit, you cannot rest. You have such a love for others, and the Holy Spirit keeps you busy reading, studying, praying, and witnessing about Jesus. How we loved every minute of it!

This wonderful elixir of life made us look around at the loose ends we had left scattered in our lives. We also had a new spiritual burden for young people trapped by occult practices.

By the time Sue and I received the Baptism, I had already given my testimony of how Christ delivered me from occult bondage at Jesus People coffeehouses in Coronado, La Mesa, and San Diego in addition to giving it at two Baptist churches and an Assembly of God church.

But now we had a new burden to really dig into the occult scene and learn how to counsel young people who had been caught in occult bondage.

Months later, through Dick Handley, we met Dave Balsiger, a former feature writer and photographer for the *Anaheim Bulletin*, who had just completed an assignment as public relations consultant for Melodyland Christian Center and was at work on an extensive research project into the occult.

Sue and I were sharing our mini-anti-occult ministry with Dave and his wife Janie one evening, when we got into a heavy discussion.

"The problem is that too many people think witchcraft is fun and games—completely harmless but, it is not!" I told them.

"That's right, Mike," Dave said. "We discovered that occult practitioners open themselves to mental derangement, criminal tendencies and possible self-destruction or the destruction of other persons."

"Yes, you're right," I said in agreement. "I saw that first hand when I was involved in the occult."

"Mike, have you considered getting out of the Navy? Giving your whole life to Christ? Making your anti-occult ministry a full-time occupation?"

"It's not that easy, Dave. You are forgetting that I reenlisted, received a cash bonus, and the Navy has been sending me through cardio-pulmonary school. I'll graduate in about a month," I told him, thinking of all the insurmountable details preventing me from going into full-time ministry. "Since you have never been in the military, you don't know how they operate. They aren't going to let me out four years early—that's crazy! Sometimes a person can get out a few months early if he is going into the police force. But if I go to Navy officials and tell them the Holy Spirit told me that the Navy should release me early so I can minister to those entrapped by the occult, they will laugh me right into the psycho ward."

"Mike, you and Sue pray about it. If it is the Lord's will, He will get you out of the Navy," Dave assured me.

We all prayed before Dave and Janie left that night, but I never really gave his impossible suggestion much real consideration.

Up until this time, I probably had been using the Navy as an excuse for not really doing the Lord's work—it was not that I did not want to follow the Lord's will, but I did not yet have the confidence to take that "faith" step into a ministry, and the Navy was a convenient reason for delaying such a decision. Ministering on Sunday was okay, but full time?

Well, if I had to be in the Navy, helping heal sick sailors and their dependents was the best possible slot for me, and I never for one minute regretted what I was doing. "But," I kept asking myself, "what sense does it make for me to help save the lives of heart patients during the week, when I could be ministering to the heart?" I wanted to be going around to churches and on the streets, witnessing to occultists, telling them what Christ had done for me. My work at the hospital kept getting in the way of my crusading—I mean, getting out there all the time and blowing the lid off this occult bit.

It is true that I did have many chances to testify to military personnel and patients, but my heart—and I began to feel my call—was elsewhere.

"Precious Savior," I prayed one day, concerning my work. I was in a place familiar to me on occasions like this, the place where I got my start as a born-again Christian—in the broom closet.

I had prayed for about fifteen minutes when a janitor opened the door, reached in, grabbed my arm, and then jumped back as if he had been shot. "What the——?" He shook his head. "Hey, what're you doin', doc, giving yourself a shot?"

"Yeah, man," I said, coming out fast. "I was getting loaded with the Holy Spirit."

"Hey, I'm with you," the janitor said. "Didn't kill the whole bottle, did you?"

"No, man, there's no end to Jesus' Spirit."

He looked at me kind of funny and edged into the closet and got a squeegee mop. "Got to shine those floors good, doc," he said, backing out and turning around. "But you got some strong stuff, I bet."

Maybe he got a message from this, too.

Some time later Sue and I were at the Speakmans' home in San Diego for a Bible study. Each of us had several turns at leading off with prayers, and then we picked up our Bibles and started reading. We had special passages we were anxious to share with one another.

Diane read the verses having to do with Jesus resurrecting Lazarus, in John 11, and concluded with, " 'Then they took away the stone from the place where the dead was laid. And Jesus lifted up his eyes, and said, "Father, I thank thee that thou hast heard me. And I knew that thou hearest me always: but because of the people which stand by I said it, that they may believe that thou hast sent me." And when he thus had spoken, he cried with a loud voice, "Lazarus, come forth." And he that was dead came forth, bound hand and foot with grave-clothes: and his face was bound about with a napkin. Jesus saith unto them, "Loose him, and let him go." ' Well?" Diane looked around.

I said, "You know what it means, Sue?"

"He's telling us that even though our cause looks hopeless, even though all these people around us seem to be condemned to hell, there's still time for Jesus to rescue them through us."

"I wonder how much time there is for mankind," I said, "before judgment."

Now began a mad scramble, a marathon to find scriptural evidence of the signs of His coming. But the verses which gave me a boost in the next problem Sue and I were to tackle were, *For the time will come when they will not endure sound doctrine; but after their own lusts shall they heap to themselves teachers, having itching ears; And they shall turn away their ears from the truth, and shall be turned unto fables* (II Tim. 4:4-4); and *Now the Spirit speaketh expressly, that in the latter times some shall depart from the faith, giving heed to seducing spirits, and doctrines of devils* (I Tim. 4:1).

Sue suddenly looked up from her Bible and suggested we spend some time studying Scriptures dealing with the occult. "Here's one," she said. "In Deuteronomy, chapter 18, verses 10-12: *There shall not be found among you any one that maketh his son or his daughter to pass through the fire, or that useth divination, or an observer of times, or an enchanter, or a witch, Or a charmer, or a consulter with familiar spirits, or a wizard, or a necromancer. For all that do these things are an abomination unto the Lord: and because of these abominations, the Lord thy God doth drive them out from before thee.*"

"I found one!" I shouted. "Isaiah, 47:13-14, *Thou art wearied in the multitude of thy counsels. Let now the astrologers, the stargazers, the monthly prognosticators, stand up, and save thee from these things that shall come upon thee. Behold, they shall be as stubble; the fire shall burn them; they shall not deliver themselves from the power of the flame: there shall not be a coal to warm at, nor fire to sit before it.*"

"Astrologers are the stargazers!" Sue pointed out. "They forecast the future. *And* divine the heavens!"

"That reminds me of something," I said, as I went to my briefcase to get out a book I had picked up earlier that day from a brother who had underlined some parts on the occult for me to read. "Father Edwin Healy, one of the best-known authorities on Catholic moral theology states, 'the Catholic church and Christians in general teach against occult practices under the first commandment—"You shall have no other gods before me." ' "

"I never thought of using the first commandment in occult counseling," Diane said. "What does he say about occultism?"

"He spends thirty pages in his book, *Moral Guidance*, talking about 'Forbidden Forms of Worship' which includes the whole occult scene," I explained.

"Father Healy states that 'astrology claims the power of accurately predicting the free future—those happenings that depend on the exercise of man's free will. Now such knowledge is unknown to all except God.'

" 'And so astrologers reading the free future in the stars, try to adorn themselves with a divine attribute. It is against the doctrine of free will, for it leads to a fatalistic view. Astrologers contend that all things happen according to a predetermined fate which can be read in one's horoscope. Hence no matter how one tries to avoid this or that, his attempts are in vain because his fate has been sealed years ago by the stars. It is against belief in divine providence, for according to astrology, God is not guiding us and helping us by his grace through the trials of temptation. If we were to judge by what astrologers teach, prayer would be fruitless and without purpose. The church has always condemned the false teaching of judicial astrology.' "

Having made the Church's position on astrology clear, Father Healy went on to point out that in all forms of divination a person can call on Satan directly or indirectly.

" 'Divination is the art of learning hidden events, particularly future hidden events that depend upon either expressly or passively appealing to Satan. But what about this passive appeal to Satan? You don't do it in so many expressed words but by virtue of the circumstances where divine enlightenment cannot reasonably be expected, we go ahead and try to discover hidden knowledge through means that are naturally inadequate for furnishing such knowledge. For example, a naturally inadequate means by which we try to learn future events is by gazing into crystal globes. So the Church has always been opposed to all of this.' "

"That sure is putting it into everyday language," Tom said.

"Say, it's apparent that astrologer Jeane Dixon, who claims to be a devout Catholic, does not know her theology very well, for based on those statements, the Catholic faith and her astrological practices are not compatible," Sue said.

"What does the Bible say about reincarnation or, as the spiritualists say, passing over," inquired Diane, who had told us earlier in the evening that she had a neighbor who claimed to be a spiritualist medium.

Sue was ready to tear into that challenge. "Turn to Hebrews 9:27, which states, *And as it is appointed unto men once to die, but after this the judgment . . .*"

"Hey, that's a good Scripture for dealing with the reincarnationist," Tom exclaimed, "but how do you deal with the occultist who says there is more than one way to God?"

"I was hit with that one two weeks ago," I commented. "I used I Timothy 2:5 which states, *For there is one God, and one mediator between God and men, the man Christ Jesus.* And of course, the *only* way to the Father is *through* the Son."

The Bible study went on like this into the early hours of morning, and it helped me overcome a hang-up I had had about taking a strong stand against organized witchcraft. I had felt somewhat uneasy about taking a strong public position, because shortly after my conversion, someone called me a radical witch-hunter who would start another terrible witch-hunt like they had in the Middle Ages.

In medieval times and the seventeeth century, the indiscriminate and widespread efforts to purge society of witches by witch-hunters did more harm than the few genuine witches who dared to operate during such a reign of terror.

Unfortunately, the modern liberated society we live in has been so disgusted with the witch-hunters of former times, the modern sophisticated person finds it difficult to believe that witches are to be taken seriously today.

We have been told so vividly that the victims of the old witch trials were helpess, harmless, old women, or perhaps innocent young children, that we are led to believe that the entire witchcraft thing was nothing but mass paranoia on the part of the Establishment of those times.

A modern American who does not know any better, hearing about today's witches, would probably chuckle and imagine a bunch of nude freaks out under the full moon doing relatively harmless things. "Okay, so there still are witches today," he might say. "But it's no big thing. We're too intelligent in the twentieth century to be frightened by misguided fanatics. Live and let live. Let them have their nude orgies. They don't affect me."

Even if witchcraft in the earlier days was innocent, which it was not, lots of occult groups *now* are fully justifying the fears of modern-day witch-hunts. Drug pushers and political revolutionists are using devil worship as a way to rake in millions of dollars, weaken the government, and destroy law enforcement.

Maybe I seem to be over-reacting, but have a look at an article by McCandlish Phillips,* a staff news writer for the *New York Times:*

> Satan is at work today in the United States and in the world with an intensity unmatched in our experience.
> And the Scriptures warn that his activity will be stepped up greatly among the nations, both in degree and in velocity, in the years immediately ahead. Satan desires to organize mankind for its own destruction.
> Unless we know of him and how he works, we will be caught short and unable to cope with the events that descend upon us. To a degree that is already the case. Supernaturalism has come into this country in a rush and it is here to stay, whether we like it or not.
> Wearing blinders will not help. Americans need desperately to know what the Bible says about it, before tragedy strikes homes and families who don't know what is happening to young members, or why.

* McCandlish Phillips, *The Bible, The Supernatural and The Jews* (New York: World Publishing Company, 1970).

I knew what we had to do. If I had truly known about Christ when I was first tempted into witchcraft, I would have turned the other way. I now had to make others see that this sort of thing could happen to them, too, and not only that, but that they were risking eternal damnation.

There is no one *down there* to lead you out. Once you're in hell, you've had it. That's it. Once you're there, it's too late. When you stop to think of *forever* . . . when you stop to think of the torment of hell . . . In hell, there is no hope. You are going to be separated from God forever. It is part of the payoff. You will hear the word "sucker" as I heard it when I first joined the Navy, but there's no discharge from hell. You are a sucker—forever.

Sure, I was saving lives now and then; I helped heal people; and I had a good thing going with my career. But what was the use of saving a few lives during my working years, if a thousand times as many human beings were being misled into eternal damnation—the living death of hell itself?

I made my decision to seek an early release from the Navy after graduating from cardio-pulmonary technician's school and being reassigned to the Oakland Naval Hospital.

A big handicap was that I had served only two years of a six-year *re*-enlistment and had already been paid a bonus for "shipping over." Not only had they invested this money in me, but I had just graduated from one of the Navy's most prestigious and expensive schools. It was a highly regarded, fully accredited school, and credit earned there could apply toward a degree at numerous colleges in the United States.

From the Navy's point of view, they had spent all this money and effort on me and were finally on the verge of recouping some of it during the next four years.

It was not as though I was goofing off, either. I had assisted on more than 50 open-heart surgeries; had helped diagnose more than 400 heart patients with chronic heart disease; made tests on blood to see how lungs were operating—how the blood was being oxygenated and how it was constituted. I had helped with pulmonary functions tests on chronic lung patients so doctors could diagnose the results.

The heart work I had done was in the diagnostic procedure called the heart cardiac catheterization, where a tube is run up an artery or vein into the heart so that they could inject dyes which would show up in X rays. By watching the picture and noting how and where the dye flows within the heart, they could detect holes in the heart, congenital defects, and things like that.

It was interesting, rewarding work, and if I had not felt called to the ministry, I would have gladly continued in it. I was happy and proud of my skills. Precisely because I *was* skilled and experienced in this highly technical field, with an excellent service record to boot, the Navy was all the less likely to let me out.

To make matters worse, my *reason* for wanting out sounded ridiculous and absurd—to get out of the United States Navy to fight Satanic spirits. Technically, the only way to obtain such a release was to claim the status of a conscientious objector, which I most surely was, though I would have been willing to serve out my hitch, had I not felt God calling me to His ministry. There were so few born-again Christians in the Navy that there wasn't the remotest chance I'd be released.

Everyone I talked to said it couldn't be done. "You're out of your gourd, Mike, for even thinking of it," one guy said. "There's just *no way*."

My superior, Dr. Francis Johnson, let me take some leave in January, 1972, to design and build the world's first "Anti-Occult Witchmobile" display for a San Diego evangelist. While Dave and I worked together, I told him what people were saying about my chances of getting out. He blinked when I described the obstacles. "It's impossible!" he said.

I shrank to pint size.

"So . . . let's start tomorrow."

I stared at him.

"Walking on water was impossible, too," Dave smiled. "But in Christ, *all* things are possible."

First, we had to decide whether to take a political or a military approach. Full of fire, we drafted a letter to Congressman Del Clawson before we had fully reckoned with the mystique of the military, although with six years of service behind me, I should have known better. When you go over the gourd of your immediate superior in the military and, particularly when you go over and *out* of the service into the civilian, especially the political sphere for a grievance or for almost anything, you are asking for trouble.

And your actions, if you are dealing with a government agency or politician are recorded in your permanent military record. The request and the response are both there in living black-and-white for every and all officers to see from here to eternity. Well, the fat was in the fire, for Congressman Clawson had already responded promptly to my request.

Of course, for our purposes, the Navy's answer to Congressman Clawson's letter in my behalf was all-important and, *had it been favorable*, all this other effect would have been nothing. I would be out, man!

The trouble was, no precedent had been set for anyone to get out of the Navy to fight Satanic spirits, and the Department of the Navy's answer was a big, fat *no*—a *no* that would be haunting me, staring up at each and every officer and clerk who would sift through my records during my more normal activities in seeking a discharge.

I was licked from the start. "It *is* impossible," I told Dave as he made preparations to leave Oakland the next day for pressing business in San Diego. "I'm beaten."

Dave stared at me a long moment. "If you think you are, then you are." He shrugged. "If you don't trust the Lord. . . ."

He had me there. I was supposed to be doing the Lord's will, wasn't I? I was not licked unless it was God's will that I be licked. And so, we picked up the pieces and started again.

The first thing we did was write to as many people as we could think of, including ministers, asking that they put our situation on their prayer list and to write letters of recommendation testifying to what I had already achieved in witnessing to get kids off dope and out of the occult. Even Sue wrote a letter of recommendation for me.

The process of getting interviews and letters from people *within* the service was coordinated by the personnel office under the management of Chief Riddle. When I first saw him, the Chief said, "Warnke, why don't you wait a couple of months? Please? We're swamped with paperwork here. Wait till things slack off, will you?" His tone seemed to indicate that what he was really saying was, "Why don't you just put it off for a while and you'll probably forget the whole thing."

"I can't do that, Chief," I countered, in a now-or-never burst of determination. "But, if you like, I could type it for you at home?"

The Chief coughed and scratched his head. I guess no one had tried that tack with him before. But I could see he still thought I was a bit sea-sick in the head.

Despite the fact that he was in total disagreement with the whole thing and absolutely certain that it did not stand a chance of being approved by Washington, he was an efficient Chief and he cooperated by helping me get everything set up—scheduling interviews, telling me how to fill out all the various forms, duplicates, triplicates and adinfinitumcates.

But he could not help showing his skepticism. "It just can't be done," he would tell me periodically when I would go in for another armload of forms or some signatures or something. "What you're trying to do is get the United States Navy involved in spiritual warfare and, that's just not in the manual."

But this light kidding did not hide the fact that he respected me for my tenacity and my service record. He knew where I had been and the blood in those Vietnam rice paddies I had waded in.

Not all of the clerks in the office knew this or cared.

One guy in particular gave me a hard time. I had to get a certain form from him and I stopped by his desk for it, in my work uniform that did not even show my rank, though he knew it already. He was an E-6, one grade higher than my E-5, which means one more stripe—equivalent to a staff sergeant in the Army or Marine Corps, compared with my buck sergeant.

As he took his own sweet time, pretending he could not find the form, he mouthed off—"Actually, I think you're just a plain coward. You're just chicken to go to Vietnam and you're trying to save your cookies by using God as a crutch."

In earlier days, I would have grabbed him out of his chair and given him a trip to fist city. Now, I just stood with my blood pressure rising and concentrated my eyes on the single, lonely ribbon on his dress jumper, the ribbon showing he had successfully completed boot camp, and smiled.

A gruff cough told us both that someone else was on the scene. I turned around. Chief Riddle was standing there. "I heard what you said, Mac. Before you go any further, you might be interested to know that Warnke happens to have eight service medals, six for service in Vietnam. He's already had three years combat with the Marine Corps. So . . ." he moved in close, never taking his eyes from his face, "I would suggest that you stow that bilge. If there's a reason Warnke wants out, it's not because he's chicken."

I took a hint from this episode and from then on, every time I went to see someone after that, I wore my dress jumper with my ribbons splashed all over it.

Dave, meanwhile, had helped me gather the evidence of my Christian beliefs and activities from other than Naval sources—letters of recommendation, newspaper and magazine clippings, summaries of radio and TV coverage of our ministry.

Other than my own statement, the first major Naval endorsement I needed was from my own immediate superior, Dr. Francis Johnson, Head of the Pulmonary Disease Branch of the Oakland Naval Hospital. Despite the fact that Dr. Johnson and I had become good friends, that he knew of my religious convictions and had authorized frequent leaves for me to conduct my ministerial activities, I knew that Dr. Johnson would have to put the Navy ahead of Warnke.

He asked me to see him at his home for the endorsement interview, and I kept telling myself the setting had no bearing on what decision he would reach. I took the testimonies and recommendations from ministers that Dave and I had gathered so far and, while I sat in his living room, he went through some of this silently. When I was about ready to climb the walls, he finally looked up and said, "Mike?"

"Yes, sir?"

"Do you know what you're doing?"

"Yes, sir, I do."

"Are you sure this is how you want to spend your life?"

"Yes, sir."

He thought a moment, then took his time asking more questions, and finally stood up. "I'll have to think about all this. I want to give it my fair consideration," he said. "Not only as your friend, but as a Naval officer, too. I have to be impartial in this matter."

I tried not to appear sea-sick as I walked to the door.

The several days I waited to see what kind of letter he would give me seemed like eternity. Then, finally, he called me in to show it to me and give me a copy.

To whom it may concern:

HM2 Warnke has worked in my department for several months. He is a well-trained cardiopulmonary technician and always performs his duties in an exceptional manner.

I have known of his ministerial work in evangelism groups for some time, and of his participation in a religious convention in San Diego. He has expressed his deep desire to go into the ministry full time and also his personal opposition to war, especially after his participation in the Viet Nam war.

I am well acquainted with Michael and his family and believe that he has sincere, irreproachable convictions about pursuing his spiritual ministry. I would like to see that he could be free to fulfill this desire as soon as possible.

Sincerely,
Francis C. Johnson, M.D.
LCDR/MC/USN
Head, Pulmonary Disease Branch
USNH Oakland, Ca.

Ever hear the Hallelujah Chorus go off inside your head? I couldn't believe it! Over and over, I thanked Jesus for standing near Dr. Johnson's shoulder. It took a lot for him to write that letter. He stuck his neck way out for me, and his fellow officers might well criticize him.

Dave was as happy as I was, but he warned me not to be overly optimistic. "That's just one hurdle, remember that, Mike," he commented.

The next was an interview with the base chaplain, Senior Chaplain Commander Ralph G. Caldwell, at the hospital. I went into his office in a hospital robe this time, because for several days *I* was a patient—with a sinus infection. Immediately, I sensed Chaplain Caldwell was a nice guy. Which, again, did not mean anything as far as what kind of recommendation he would give me, I kept reminding myself. I told him about being in the occult ministry.

"Oh, really?" he responded. "I'm really interested in that, because I've had several people in here who were involved in the occult." He went on to relate the case of a girl who had been in to see him a week before. She had been snared by the promises of a medium in San Francisco. Now the medium, using fear tactics, was holding the chick up for a bunch of money. The medium had her frightened to death. "I can't seem to convince the girl that there's nothing to worry about," he complained.

"If you'll pardon me, Chaplain, I think it's because there *is* something to worry about. It's the real thing."

"Well, how do *you* think I could help her?" he asked.

"She's got to confess Christ, confess her occult sins and then ask for repentance and the power of the Holy Spirit to counteract Satan," I said, going on to elaborate our program for defeating Satan.

The chaplain thought for a moment and said, "I'll try it. No one had ever explained the occult to me like you have." Thank you, Jesus, for the perfect opening! "Sir, the reason I came in here is that I need to get out of the service, to go into the anti-occult ministry full time. What shall I do?"

He took a few moments registering what I had said, then advised, "I'll tell you what you're going to do. You're going to stay in the Navy and serve your hitch, because there's absolutely no way for you to get out. No precedent . . ."

There was that word again! I was sick of hearing it, although I knew I needed to be reminded constantly of the insane thing I was doing.

But Chaplain Caldwell wasn't finished. "You know, Mike, even if I were to give you a favorable recommendation, which remains extremely doubtful, and even if several other officers around here support your application, I'm afraid that wouldn't necessarily mean that you'd get it. Keep this in mind to avoid disappointment in the future: the petition still has to go to *Washington*."

"Well, Chaplain Caldwell," I said morosely, my throat dry, "all I want is the Lord's will. If it's His will for me to stay in the service, I will. If not, you know I'm going to get out regardless of what the precedents are."

But the chaplain's tone and pessimism hit hard. After all, he probably knew more about conscientious objection to service on religious grounds than anyone else in the entire hospital, including the whole personnel office lumped together. For him to be completely down on my chances was a bitter blow. I got the creepy feeling that, as God's representative on the base, he was right this minute being used by the Lord to tell me it was not His will that I be released.

It was only later, after I had shaken the dark mood, that I realized the possible significance of Chaplain Caldwell's action. He had been in the Navy since forever and was a personal friend of Admiral Nimitz and Admiral Halsey. He had been around. For him to give me a favorable recommendation, regardless of how effective it might be with the bright, new brass controlling things now, would be a tremendous plus. And he did.

To Whom It May Concern:

This is to certify that I have interviewed HM2 Michael WARNKE regarding his religious beliefs and convictions as they relate to his request for Conscientious Objector status.

My first session with WARNKE was during his brief hospitalization on the EENT Ward. I was immediately made aware of his deep religious commitment and involvement in the anti-occult ministry. Subsequently I have talked at length with WARNKE specifically concerning his religious, moral and philosophical views regarding duty in a combatant military organization. It is my estimate that WARNKE'S position as a conscientious objector slowly evolved during his duty with Marines, in a combat situation, and has crystallized in the last few months. He sincerely feels there is now no alternative course of action but to process this request.

WARNKE does not object to the employment of a military service and other forms of protection for the preservation of good order and discipline in the world but he feels he can no longer, in good conscience, be an active participant in an organization which could involve taking human life.

I believe WARNKE is highly motivated from a sincere moral and spiritual commitment and so recommend favorable consideration of his request for Conscientious Objector status.

RALPH G. CALDWELL
CDR, CHC, USN
Senior Chaplain

And He shall reign for ever and ever! The next stop was the psychiatrist's office. The Navy insisted on this examination as part of my obstacle course to complete my application for c. o. status because, given the fact that most people in the Navy are merely nominal Christians if they are Christians at all, when you take a real stand for God in the Navy, they think there is some kind of insecurity inside you—that your gourd has some rattling marbles in it.

Lieutenant Commander R. H. Cain was a professional psychiatrist, and he had full access to all my service records. Despite much prayer and my faith in prayer, I was jittery when I went into his office and was seated in the usual red-padded chair in the dimly-lit consultation room. He started out like a true professional—except, perhaps, in not masking his conviction that I might be a few bricks shy of a full load. This impression was intensified when I started talking about wanting to fight spirits instead of human beings.

I had to spill my guts about everything.

"So, in Catholic school, you got a kind of hang-up with all the ritual? It really turned you on?"

I nodded and he wrote something down in a pad he was trying to conceal from my view. "You prayed a lot to the images? Do you mean it literally when you say you spent 'hours' on your knees in prayer?"

I shrugged. "I didn't time myself."

"Mike, did you ever talk to God?"

"Yes, sir."

"Does he ever . . . *answer?*"

"Yes, sir. He does."

"How often is this?"

"Every day, sir."

He cocked his head, staring directly at me for a moment, instead of trying to observe my features without *appearing* to. "Well, have you ever *seen* Him?"

"Yes, sir. I have."

"You must be some kind of Pentecostal!"

"Yes, sir, I am."

"What do you believe in?"

I waved my hand. "Oh, healing, tongues, all the charismatic gifts—the gifts of the Holy Spirit. The Power of the Blood. The Bible."

I was exhausted emotionally. All I wanted to do was go

home and rack out for a week. But I still had to endure the wrap-up of the examination as he sat in his leather chair, pondering, trying to think if he had missed anything. Finally, he said, "Warnke, I'm going to have to take this and think about it, because I have to determine whether you've been having delusions or whether yours is a real experience."

So, I waited. Again. Waited, hoped, prayed. I went about my duties in a mechanical manner, careful in conducting the tests I was asked to give, obedient, showing compassion for patients I helped the doctors diagnose. And dying. Just dying inside.

Then, one day, as I was putting some testing equipment away, I heard my name being called. "Personnel wants to see ya," a guy told me. I rushed down to the personnel office. "Letter for you," the clerk said nonchalantly.

I ripped open the envelope. It was my copy of the psychiatrist's report. I bored holes into it with my eyes, impatiently skimming over the unimportant details.

The report summarized my Christian endeavors during the past six years, and included the statement, "His conviction of incompatibility of his beliefs and military service began during his combat experience in Vietnam and has increased to the present." Dr. Cain had even understated things when he said, "He has a moderate degree of concern regarding his CO application, but this is not to an excessive degree." In actual fact, I was chewing my nails down to my second knuckle.

I scanned the bit about my childhood and the Satanist experiences and stopped to re-read the statements near the conclusion—"He is convinced of the religious validity of healing, speaking in tongues and his true experience with Christ. In this individual these do not represent delusional concern."

King of Kings, and Lord of Lords!

I read on. Surely in the summary, Dr. Cain would come out with it, like, "Actually, Mike Warnke is a raving maniac and should be confined indefinitely for observation."

What it really said was, "The patient is an intelligent,

articulate individual who has a history of a long term and deep religious commitment. There is no evidence of any acute psychiatric disorder."

I felt dizzy. If getting out of the service on a c. o. to engage in spiritual warfare was a major miracle, part of it had already been achieved, because this examination report was certainly a minor miracle.

It had to be the Lord's work, persuading Dr. Cain to give me a good report. But I was not through worrying, yet. In the back of my mind kept ringing the words of Chaplain Caldwell ". . . it still has to be approved by *Washington*."

Now that I had all the paperwork collected, the next and hopefully last step was compiling it and sending it to Washington with the proper instrument of transmittal. This was a procedure for which I needed the help of the Legal Officer. When I went to his office, apparently obligated to do his duty, he spent nearly an hour trying to dissuade me from going any further on such a hopeless mission. "Besides, just think of what you stand to lose, Warnke, not to mention all the enemies you'll be making." He began a long series of examples and concluded with, "Even your veteran administration rights may go down the tube."

I remained firm.

He coughed nervously. "Well, it's too late to start the process today. Come back first thing Monday morning. If you haven't changed your mind."

When I saw Lieutenant Kahn Monday morning, we were both feeling better and really got down to the nitty gritty. He was a representative of the Admiral and he would sign by direction of the Commanding Officer, once we got the transmitting document finalized. It turned out that Lieutenant Kahn was not a bad guy at all except on Fridays. In fact, he was very interested in the occult ministry. "You believe in demons?" he asked.

I nodded.

He went on to say he had read something about LeVey's outfit and some of the weird things that were going on. He wanted me to fill him in. "Why do you think witchcraft is such a serious threat?" he asked. "Isn't it really more like a game kids and old ladies play?"

"Yeah," I answered. "Like Russian Roulette." I had to explain that I believe Man is a spiritual being. In life, you are governed by spiritual forces. Whether you like it or not, you are governed by either good forces or evil forces.

We spent a lot of time talking, with me answering questions about myself for the application, and questions about the occult for Lieutenant Kahn. I had to explain what I meant by "devil," the "occult," and a bunch of other words.

He seemed to take it all in. Then, finished, he looked me square in the eye. "Well, I don't know how good your case is for c. o., but I think your ministry is worthwhile. It has a lot to offer. You've convinced me there's a threat, and I'm sure you and your friends are on the right track."

There was a lot of clerical work left to be done on the basic document he had just sketched in, but everyone in the office really pitched in. His secretary, Mrs. Taylor, took a special interest and got the paperwork out fast. When it was in final form at last, it all went to BuPers, the Bureau of Naval Personnel, in Washington.

There was more than enough to do in the meantime to keep my mind off getting the answer but, I could not help getting periodically depressed. I had seen things like this happen before. You put your whole soul into it, you sweat blood and cry. You work until you ache and your stomach is all twisted and you have such a painful desire for a good outcome that you can taste it. Then, the old whammie! A cold, stabbing *no*. A shaft.

I prayed the hardest I had ever prayed for anything in my life, but I was really without hope. Who was I, after all, to assume that the Lord would single me out, anyway —Michael Warnke, ex-Satanist—with all the sins I had committed and stuff I had done, for this very special *miracle*, this unprecedented favor? At least, I would be in the life-saving business and, if I had Dr. Johnson for a boss for the next four years, I would probably get enough time off to help a lot of kids, at that. It would not be all that bad, when you get right down to it.

I was resigned to a flat *no*, and when I got a call from one of the chicks in personnel that something very official looking from Washington had arrived for me and would I please come down and pick it up, I knew it was the formal denial of my request.

I went down to get it and started to shove it in my jumper pocket when the chick said, "Aren't you going to open it?"

"What's the use?" I muttered. But I opened it to satisfy her. It wasn't the *no*, but it certainly was not a *yes*, either. It was another big, fat, useless headache, like the kind they advertise on TV, but there were not enough aspirins in the whole hospital to get rid of this headache.

Chapter Fourteen

During the initial lining-up of interviews and examinations I had been given the option of being interviewed by a line officer. Dave and I had grabbed at the chance to avoid being interrogated by such a hard-nosed military type. But now Washington said, "If you want us to give your application consideration, you must be interviewed by a line officer." It did not seem fair of them to change their minds like that, but there was nothing I could do about it. This development made me all the more certain of defeat, and the officer chosen by the Command to talk with me did not help matters any. Sure enough, he was a hard-core career officer and, to make matters as dismal as possible, he was a lieutenant bucking for promotion. He was military from the word *go*.

On the credit side, he was not belligerent and appeared to be a real nice guy. He treated me decently and listened carefully to everything I had to say. But I could tell from the very beginning he was against the whole idea. The Navy, in his book, came first, foremost and always—ahead of every other commitment. It did not bother his conscience that he served in the military, and he could not understand why it did anyone else.

He did not give me a hard time or anything. He was helpful and understanding and I liked him, and we developed a kind of friendship. But it was like a doctor examining you for cancer: I could tell from his expression what his diagnosis would be, and it merely confirmed my recent misgivings and hopelessness. When I did get to see the letter, my fears were justified: All he had conceded was that I serve in the continental U.S.A. only but that I continue medical duties in the Navy until my hitch was up.

I was certain he had given my application a death blow but Dave kept trying to encourage me and remind me that the h.ghest court of appeal was still to be heard from even after Washington got this supplement to my application. "What's that, Dave?" I asked, thinking he had ideas of taking the whole thing to the Supreme Court and shuddering at the monumental task it would be to prepare a case before that august body.

"Jesus Christ," Dave replied.

And so I released the whole thing to Him in prayer, claimed His peace, and asked Him to give me a glad and peaceful heart—whatever the outcome. With that prayer, all my fretting and striving ceased. My whole attitude changed. I was content to live in the here and now without being agitated about what some tomorrow would bring. Why couldn't I just as well make a name as the "Gospel-preaching naval medic from Oakland, who healed bodies by day and soul by night"? The more I thought this over, the better it sounded. And I was indeed able to put it into practice . . . to the extent that I became reconciled to staying in—happy, in fact, to be doing His work in His will. There was certainly plenty to do, and I hardly realized how many weeks were going by.

One afternoon, as I was in the Duty Office, doing some paperwork and keeping an ear on the telephone, I was wondering if I could wangle a radio or even TV program, maybe something like "The Occult and God," in which I would interview dopers and Satanists and then give my plug for Jesus Christ as the answer to their troubles.

The phone shrilled. "Cardio-Pulmonary. Warnke speaking. May I help you?"

"Warnke? This is the personnel office. We have a letter down here, authorizing your discharge."

"Hunh?"

"Is this HM2 Warnke? Michael Warnke?"

"Yes. Yes. Yes."

"Well, I have a *letter* down here authorizing your discharge on CO basis."

"You've got to be kidding."

"I'm not kidding."

"You're . . . you're *kidding!*"

"I'm *not*. Really. It's from the Bureau of—"

I went nuts. I laughed and cried. I finally calmed down enough to say, "I'll be there in a minute to sign the papers. Don't let them out of your sight."

I hung up and started crying. My friends and co-workers came in. "Hey, we heard you from the other office. What's wrong?"

"I'm out."

They shouted and carried on, patting me on the back, shaking their heads in disbelief, shaking my hand until I thought my arm would come off. "Hey, Warnke, what's the secret? How did you do it?"

I backed away from them, pointed heavenward, and turned and ran down to personnel, shaking like a leaf in a whirlwind.

"You can get out in seven days," the girl said.

I was mighty tempted. Then, I thought better of it. "Can I finish up this month so I can get a full paycheck? Is it possible to get my discharge on, let's see . . . hmm . . . the second of June?"

She nodded. She was trying not to smile, but she mirrored some of my utter jubilation.

I started processing that same afternoon. It was almost as involved as the processing for making the application, but not nearly as nerve-racking—knowing that there was now no doubt. I made an appointment to get my physical, check out, dropped by special services so that they could be sure that I had not gotten away with anything like tennis balls or whatever. I returned my overdue books to the base library and made the rounds of friends to let them know what was going on.

I had to see several officers and get my records out of

storage and take them down and have them dictated and closed. The process of getting out took two weeks altogether, but it was a real blessing, with everyone kidding me, showing their happiness for me. I had called Dr. Johnson the day I got word, and he was quiet for a while, then said, "You can see that the Lord still does miracles. Even today."

Everyone was deeply impressed with the Lord's hand in all of this. What I consider best of it all was that there were guys in the office who had watched me all the way through the whole thing, all the time sympathizing with me but totally skeptical of my chances, especially the long-timers. I had told them time after time that if I got out, it would be God's work.

"I believe it's God's will, and I'm praying every night that He'll get me out so I can go into his ministry—if it's His will."

"It will never happen," they would say.

Now, it *had* happened, and they were given a real witness of God's power—that it still works and is vital to everyday things and to *everyone's* life, no matter who you are.

On June 2, Sue and I packed up our dollies and dishes and split to San Diego. We floated down there on Cloud Nine for sure, this time—the real article. We thanked God every mile of the way. Even after I had been reconciled to not getting out of the Navy, in my prayers I had sneaked in words like, "but I hope it *is* Your will that I be released." God had answered our prayers, and I felt happy that, during those last few weeks, I had relaxed and let Him take over.

Sue and I settled down in a tiny house and began to get organized. We started calling people to set up speaking engagements and get some sort of system established to run our ministry.

In addition to giving me a release from my naval commitment, God had given me a grave responsibility. Now Sue and I were faced with the awesome challenge of fulfilling it and justifying all the fuss and faith-walking I had done to get where I was. One thing we pondered was a name for the new ministry.

"This is the end of one part of our lives," Sue said one day, "and the beginning of another."

"You know, you're right," I agreed. "And looking around and seeing all the signs foretold in the Bible that would signal the 'end times,' I'm convinced that *we*, you and I, are living in *the* end times."

"This know also, that in the last days perilous times shall come. For men shall be lovers of their own selves, covetous, boasters, proud, blasphemers, disobedient to parents, unthankful, unholy . . . lovers of pleasure . . ." Sue had tears in her eyes.

"Man, you memorize beautifully, honey. But listen, we are *beginning* a new ministry for the Lord for the end times, the anti-occult ministry. So, what did Jesus say about beginnings and ends?"

"He said, 'I am the—uh—Alpha and the Omega.' That *means* beginning and end."

"So let's call our ministry, 'The Alpha Omega Outreach.' "

Sue agreed wholeheartedly.

In essence, the Alpha Omega Outreach is Jesus Outreach, because "Alpha and Omega" is also another name for Jesus.

Dave and Janie, Sue and I got together to talk about it and make a schedule of speaking engagements which would initiate the ministry. We ran into the problem of explaining to each pastor and youth leader we spoke to the whole story—my Satanist activities, Vietnam, and finally getting out of the Navy. Ministers seemed to need exhaustive assurances that we were the real article.

"What Alpha Omega needs," Dave said, "is more publicity. You can't afford all the time it's taking to do the promotion phone by phone, letter by letter, church by church. What you need is to kick this thing off with a press conference. If enough people know about your ministry, they'll contact *you* to come to speak to their groups."

"Hey, I'm with *that!*" I said.

Dave took charge of setting up the press conference. He attracted about twenty people there, representing the wire services, radio, television, newspapers, and magazines. It was really a scene! At last I could manage to submerge the old Mike Warnke and feel I was merely an instrument of the Lord. It was God who was really getting all this publicity, and inwardly I passed it all up to Him.

They shot a million questions at me and my associates, but the questions I thought most important and that I answered most emphatically and at some length boiled down to three basic questions.

One reporter asked, "Mr. Warnke, how do you feel that you can help get people straightened out who are involved in occult practices today?"

I did not have to think long to phrase my answer to that one, because I had been saying the same thing countless times before church groups and youth organizations in California and elsewhere. "Well, I've been the whole route. I've been a Satanist, a Satanic high priest. I've had control over a lot of people. A bunch! And I've eaten human flesh and drunk human blood.

"I enslaved people and sought power in order to attain something that was so simple that I didn't even notice it. I tried all my life to find fulfillment and the meaning of life, and through black magic, man-made philosophies, and following the gods of this world, I stumbled along and pushed my way.

"I finally found there is Someone more powerful than the god of this world, and that is Jesus Christ. His philosophy is a philosophy of love rather than hate—one of what He can do for you, not what you can do for Him. It's so much easier, more wonderful, more peaceful, and more rewarding to follow Christ than to follow Satan.

"I believe that the Lord has given me the strength to share this with others."

I cleared my throat and moved a little away from the

mike. Everyone was quietly staring at me and for a moment I felt a shiver pass through me as I realized that these words seemed to come to me straight from the Lord. "During my sojourn with Satan," I continued, "I was instrumental in leading a thousand people into Satan's kingdom. Now I pray to God that He will allow our ministry to influence a thousand souls for good for every one I led into the darkness."

I noticed the reporters and others writing furiously and talking with each other after I had finished, perhaps checking on the exact wordage. Several had tape recorders, and it suddenly hit me that everything I had just said and would say would be in print.

On previous occasions when I had noticed someone staring at me because he had seen my picture and story in the *Los Angeles Times* or *Time* magazine, I had not thought much about it. Now I realized how serious it all was. Millions of people would be seeing my picture and reading about my experiences and my convictions, and I suddenly felt the full terrific weight of the responsibility to really tell it like it is. This was no poke, no game, no idle TV program.

"Uh, Mr. Warnke," a wire service representative said, "what can the average citizen do to protect himself from witchcraft and Satanic practices in his community?"

I laughed. "That's a loaded question. I don't have time to tell you all the different ways. But, first of all, you have to know that the occult is *here, now,* and a real danger. You can find out more about witchcraft and other occults as a member of a group, such as a church group, then suggest to other groups that they find out more about it and *do* something."

"With all the written material available," a reporter wryly commented, "that shouldn't be too hard."

"The trouble is, lots of the stuff is slanted," I replied. "When I first came back from Vietnam, I was amazed to see the increase on the newsstands not only of porno books and junk like that, but books on the occult. Even libraries let anyone check out witchcraft and other occult books. People could urge booksellers and librarians to impose some age limits, at least, so kids would be protected from all this trash.

"If the atheists can get prayers banned in schools, we can certainly write to government agencies like the FCC and to the school boards and state legislators to protect radio, TV, and school campuses from being used as showcases where the occult is glamorized and promoted. Man, until you get action on stopping these guys from getting to our kids, you're just plain lost."

"Any more suggestions for community action?"

I raised my eyebrows. "Enough to fill an encyclopedia. People could write letters to editors to protest against horoscopes and other features on the occult and against books which glorify the occult or make it seem attractive."

"What would you say about the Manson murders?"

"Well, the main point there is that lots of crimes are committed as a result of occult involvement, and people should report to the police if they see someone going around wearing human bones as jewelry, or if there's a group meeting under the full moon . . ."

There was some chuckling, and I shook my head and spoke up loudly: "These witchcraft rituals are where I really got going downhill fast. Lots of the stuff they do at the coven meetings are against the law, and if they know the police are watching them, maybe some of them at least will drop out. Not to mention the dope that those guys are using . . ."

I took a drink of water. "If people would just show more disapproval to store owners, too—get up-tight about store people who commercialize on occult merchandise. The same thing goes for movies—movie houses and the producers, too, who make the junk in the first place.

"You know, most service clubs—and women's clubs— are pretty conservative organizations. But sometimes even those clubs are hoodwinked when some high-sounding guy says he has a new twist to tell their members. People could

213

try to get their clubs and societies to understand that there is no such a thing as 'white' magic. *All* magic is bad news."

"What would you consider to be the most important thing people could do, Mr. Warnke?" a gray-haired man from a Los Angeles newspaper asked.

"Fight fire with fire. Go directly to the greater source of supernatural power of all. *Pray.* Pray for all of us—for humanity. And also pray for specific people who are involved in the occult. If you know of someone who's on drugs and hung up in the occult, put him on your prayer list, and hit the Lord hard every night for this person."

At this point, I could see that everyone was getting restless. Most of the newsmen thought they had gotten the main idea, that they had enough to make a good story. Yet, I had not answered the most important question of all. It had not even been asked.

"I have one or two more comments to make," I said. "I think they are important!"

Someone else in the crowd said, "One last question, Mr. Warnke: What if a person is in the occult, or is demon-possessed? Is there any way to help him or is it too late? How can someone help a person who is really trapped in this type of thing?"

This was close enough to what I had in mind to say—or, rather, to let the Lord say. I just opened my mouth, and Jesus used my tongue. "The first thing that a person has to do is confess his faith in Christ," I heard myself say. "In John 3:16-18, it says, *For God so loved the world, that he gave his only begotten Son, that whosoever believeth in him should not perish, but have everlasting life. For God sent not his Son into the world to condemn the world; but that the world through him might be saved. He that believeth on him is not condemned: but he that believeth not is condemned already, because he hath not believed in the name of the only begotten Son of God.*

"If you can get this feeling of faith and you acknowledge it—if the person involved in the occult will do this— he is making a beginning. Faith is the first weapon and

214

shield against Satan, as Hebrews points out in chapter 11, verse 6—*But without faith it is impossible to please him: for he that cometh to God must believe that he is, and that he is a rewarder of them that diligently seek him.*"

I paused so that the words would sink in. I had spoken slowly because I knew a lot of these guys had not been accustomed to listening to the Gospel, and I wanted them to get the message for themselves, as well as for their readers and/or listeners.

"Is that all there is to it?" a young redheaded guy asked.

"No. After confessing your faith in Christ, you next have to make a confession of your occult sins. You have to recognize that your involvement in the occult *is* disobeying God. You have to go right down the list of all the different occult things you have been doing and tell Jesus and ask Him to forgive you. This includes fortune-telling, dabbling in astrology—"

"Would you class playing with the Ouija board as an occult . . . *sin?*"

"Yes," I answered firmly. "Part of the basis for this is in Proverbs 28:13: *He that covereth his sins shall not prosper: but whoso confesseth and forsaketh them shall have mercy.* And in Acts 19:18-19: *And many that believed came, and confessed, and shewed their deeds. Many of them also which used curious arts brought their books together, and burned them before all men: and they counted the price of them, and found it fifty thousand pieces of silver.*"

"I have one last question," one of the reporters said, standing and getting ready to write my answer.

"Well, I have one last answer to give," I said. "Let's see if I answer your question or not. The next thing this guy has to do if he is involved in the occult is to *repent* of his sins. According to Romans 6:1 and 6—*What shall we say then? Shall we continue in sin, that grace may abound? . . . Knowing this, that our old man is crucified with him, that the body of sin might be destroyed, that henceforth we should not serve sin.* And Ephesians 4:21-22 tells us *If so be that ye have heard him, and have been taught by him, as the truth is in Jesus: That ye put off concerning the former conversation the old man, which is corrupt according to the deceitful lusts.*

"In other words," I continued, "you have to confess your faith in Christ, confess your occult sins, and repent of your sins. Then, in the name of Jesus, command Satan to depart. As a believer, you have the authority. Command the evil spirit to leave you, and do so loud and clear. Or, you can do these things for another person if that person is subjecting himself to your help. You can always pray for anybody whether he knows it or not, but it works most certainly when he wants your help. And never forget one thing, a spiritual law, more absolute than any law of physics or nature: Jesus is *always* victor.

"Now, I could go on and give you a lot more Scriptures for doing these things, but the main thing is for people who are troubled with demons or occult bondage to be willing to do something about it, and then to do these things that I have just mentioned."

The meeting broke up after that, with a couple of newsmen coming up to re-check their notes with my statistics. As we left, I sensed more than ever the truth of what Sue had said: a part of our lives was ended for good; a new adventure in Him had just begun.

It was a little frightening, going after Satan where he lived, until I remembered Who was walking beside us, and Who dwelt within us.

My back straightened, and my pace picked up, as I recalled our combat orders from the sixth chapter of Ephesians:

Finally, my brethren, be strong in the Lord, and in the power of his might. Put on the whole armour of God, that ye may be able to stand against the wiles of the devil. For we wrestle not against flesh and blood, but against principalities, against powers, against the rulers of the darkness of this world, against spiritual wickedness in high places. Wherefore take unto you the whole armour of

God, that ye may be able to withstand in the evil day, and having done all, to stand. Stand, therefore, having your loins girt about with truth, and having on the breast-plate of righteousness; And your feet shod with the preparation of the gospel of peace; Above all, taking the shield of faith wherewith ye shall be able to quench all the fiery darts of the wicked. And take the helmet of salvation and the sword of the Spirit, which is the word of God.

Any counseling requests, comments, or inquiries for speaking engagements should be directed to:

Mike Warnke
Alpha Omega Outreach
1819 East Dakota
Fresno, CA   93726

3-74

Appendix I

OCCULT INTEREST CAUSES

Although a person's quest for spiritual fulfillment is the basic cause of the current occult revival, there are other contributory factors.

The following causes are a composite of research done by many people, particularly that of British Researcher Dr. Oz Guiness, Associated Press Religion Editor George W. Cornell, and United Press Religion Editor Louis Cassels.

The causes can be summarized as follows:

1. The death of rationalism which invites the supernatural again, whether it be witches or a radical Satanist cult.
2. Disbelief in modern theology. The supernatural of the Scriptures has been secularized and watered down.
3. The influence of Eastern religions in America with its tendency to mix any and all beliefs into one melting pot.
4. The modern chaos and complexity of our society. Man is making an attempt at short-cut thinking.
5. The present state of progress in psychic and parapsychological research has motivated people toward the idea that the occult is really a science.
6. The occult has a reality to it, but seldom do people give much thought to the supernatural source of the reality.
7. Disenchantment with standard-brand churches which seem to give no alternative to the secular world.
8. Theologians obsessed with trying to prove that Christianity should only be a here-and-now aid to ethical behavior.

9. The lack of governmental regulatory control over the news media, entertainment and commercial products propagating involvement interest in the occult.
10. A personal retreat to the irrational where an individual is relieved of the responsibility of facing up to decisions personally . . . a regression to a childlike state of mind.

Appendix II

HOW TO FIGHT OCCULTISM

What can you do to fight the spreading occultism in our country? You can do many things.

First you can realize that God is the answer to the lures of Satanism. By talking to Him and asking His guidance you will be far more effective than if you go out on your own without Him to help you.

A. WRITE LETTERS—Write to your Congressman and Senators. Also write to your state legislators for they read every letter and frequently take action. Tell them what is going on and ask them to help.

Write to your newspaper. Tell them what is happening and why you object to it. Keep your letters around two hundred to three hundred words. Remember the Letters to the Editor section of daily newspapers is one of the best-read sections of the paper. Also write to radio and TV stations about the problem.

B. USE YOUR TELEPHONE—Call your newspaper editor and ask him to investigate the occult activities in your city. Also call your radio and television station and ask them to investigate too. Check to see if your Congressman or your state legislator has an office in your city and call him or his secretary to ask for a similar investigation. Call your city and county officials and ask them to take action on local problems with the occult.

C. WORK WITH YOUR CHURCH—Help the members of your church and other churches in the community to learn of the errors of the occult. Help them plan action programs to stem occult growth.

D. INVESTIGATE YOUR SCHOOLS—See what your schools are teaching. Check courses called "Mysticism" and "Literature of the Supernatural." See if teachers are pushing occult practices on students. Then take your case to the school board. Tell the newspapers, radio and television what you have found. Do not let the school administrators tell you to keep the information confidential. If it is wrong—tell the world.

E. BRING IN SPEAKERS—Obtain knowledgeable speakers on the occult to address your club or group. There are many clubs now inviting speakers on astrology and mysticism; offer them speakers on the occult who can show why it is wrong.

F. PICKET—Picket stores and movie houses that offer occult books and films. Let the public know this is wrong. Let the news media know you are picketing and why.

G. PRAY—PRAY—PRAY—Jesus is the only effective answer to those who want deliverance from the occult. God has a greater interest in halting occultism than you do. He is only waiting for you to ask Him to help you. Don the full Gospel armor, pray, and ask others to pray that He will guide you. He will!

FOR A
FREE SAMPLE COPY
OF
LOGOS JOURNAL
WRITE
BOX 191
PLAINFIELD, N.J.   07060

Redeem at Bookstore

SAVE 10¢

ON ANY LOGOS BOOK

with retail price of $1.25 or more.

MR. BOOKDEALER: Logos International will pay you the face value of this coupon, 10¢, plus 3¢ for handling, if you have received it in accordance with all the terms of this offer and if upon request you submit evidence thereof satisfactory to Logos International. Invoices proving purchases of sufficient stock within the past 90 days to cover coupons presented for redemption must be shown on request. Any sales tax must be paid by customer. This coupon may not be assigned or transferred. Offer void where prohibited, taxed or otherwise restricted. Cash redemption value 1/20 of 1¢. To redeem this coupon mail it to: Logos International, P. O. Box 191, Plainfield, NJ 07061. Limit one coupon per purchase of book. Any other use constitutes fraud.

Customer please fill out rear of coupon

10¢   **10¢**

Good in U.S.A. only

Store Coupon

Date _____

Book Store Name _____

_____

Title of Book Purchased

Using Coupon _____

_____

_____

Customer's Name

_____

Customer's Address

_____

City,   State,   Zip

SAVE TIME - fill out coupon
before presenting to store.

Coupon not completed with above
information will be invalid.